W9-AWW-320

THE SUPERMAN COMPLEX

ACHIEVING THE BALANCE
THAT LEADS TO
TRUE SUCCESS

THE SUPERMAN COMPLEX

MAX CAREY

LONGSTREET
Atlanta, Georgia

Published by
LONGSTREET, INC.
A subsidiary of Cox Newspapers
A subsidiary of Cox Enterprises, Inc.
2140 Newmarket Parkway
Suite 122
Marietta, GA 30067
www.lspress.com

Copyright © 1999 by Max Carey

All rights reserved. No part of this book may be reproduced in any form or by any means without the prior written permission of the Publisher, excepting brief quotations used in connection with reviews, written specifically for inclusion in a magazine or newspaper.

Printed in the United States of America

1st printing 1999

Library of Congress Catalog Card Number: 99-61752

ISBN: 1-56352-516-X

Jacket design by Burtch Bennett Hunter
Book design by Megan Wilson

Dedicated to

This book is dedicated to 'the wind beneath my wings'—
my sweetheart Susan . . .

For loving me when I wasn't easy to love . . .

To my dear children, Elise, Caroline, and Billy . . .

You have the wisdom to lead yourselves and others.

You have the courage to confront your peers and me.

You have the love and compassion to survive my frailties.

To my Dad who never stopped providing, never stopped teaching, and never stopped loving.

To my sister Toots who has always been the light of the Carey Family, for all of us.

To my brother Chris for being my hero and my friend.

To my brother Mike for being my friend and my hero.

And to my Mom who left us early. You had . . .

the Spirit of an Immigrant,
the Soul of a Entrepreneur,
and the Heart of a Mother.

My special thanks to Ken Labish and Barry Tarshis for shaping the concept, to Harvey Ardman for bringing it to life and, of course, to Carlene Jones, Martha Jewett, and Diane Tanger for making a dream come true.

ACKNOWLEDGMENTS

This is to thank *you*—all of my friends. You have always been there for me.

• You were my friend throughout grammar school, high school, and college—you even overlooked my flaws enough to vote for me once or twice.

• You were with me side by side on athletic fields all over the world and you were the best teammate I ever had.

• You were in the hostile skies with me and you looked out for me, even when it put your life at risk. God, you were an incredible wingman.

• You taught me my first business skills and gave me the keys to a successful professional career. You had the wisdom I needed, and you gave it so freely.

• You came to work at CRD, and you trusted and believed in me. For that I will be eternally grateful.

• You were at the CEO/Entrepreneur conferences during the dark days of CRD, and without ever realizing it you lifted me up and gave me hope.

• You were a "Vet" with a heart and you comforted me in my despair, and, through your pain, my pain was healed.

• You sat next to me in church and reached out to save me. Unselfishly your only concern was a richness and fullness in my life that is God's promise.

• You were a pal, a family member, a coach, a teammate, a wingman, a partner, a mentor, a minister, a confidant, a supporter, a teacher, an employee, and a soulmate.

• But most of all, you were a friend. You were my friend.

And if it's true that "a friend is a gift you give yourself," I have given myself the greatest gifts any man could expect to accrue in his lifetime.

So thank you. This book's for you.

Contents

THE SUPERMAN COMPLEX

Introduction

I never saw it coming.

One moment I was standing on the deck of my home in suburban Atlanta, a cup of coffee in one hand and the morning paper in the other hand. The next, I was doubled over on the edge of a chaise longue, my arms wrapped around my legs, and I was sobbing uncontrollably, the tears literally *shooting* out of my eyes as if they were being squirted from a water pistol.

The year was 1984. I was thirty-four years old, and, as far as I was consciously aware, there was absolutely no reason for me to be having any sort of emotional breakdown.

A year or so earlier, yes, my life had been in disarray. My business was in trouble. Creditors were hounding us day and night. My wife and I were constantly bickering. But just as I had done throughout my life whenever I was up against any sort of challenge and when the odds were stacked against me—whether it was on the football field, in flight school, or in the skies of Vietnam—I had refused to be cowed by adversity. I didn't panic. I didn't quit. I dug in. I grabbed hold of the reins of my business with renewed intensity and focus, and through sheer will, I was not only able to keep the business from going under, I had now begun to grow it: we now had eight employees. Our client list was expanding. Creditors were being paid off.

My personal life, too, was improving as well—or so I thought. I was taking better care of myself. And thanks, mainly, to my wife Susan, to her patience and to her faith, and to the powerful bond that we'd forged and had somehow maintained ever since we'd first met in Pensacola, Florida, thirteen years earlier, my marriage was no longer a daily battleground. Our three children, Elise, Caroline, and Billy, had become an enormous source of joy in my life.

So the logical question, of course, was why the breakdown, and why now: if things were going so well, what was I doing on this beautiful spring morning, curled up like a baby and crying my eyes out—so out of control that I couldn't catch my breath long enough to explain to my terrified wife what was going on?

Vietnam revisited

The most logical answer—and the answer Susan and I ultimately arrived at an hour or so later, once I had calmed down and was back in control—was Vietnam. That was the word I managed to scrawl on a pad near the chaise longue while I was trying to catch my breath long enough to explain to my wife why I was such an emotional basket case.

The explanation made sense. The last thing I remember before the attack hit that morning was opening up the newspaper and seeing a photograph of the Vietnam memorial that had been dedicated the day before in Washington. That photograph had evidently triggered an emotional response that I must have buried deep in my subconscious since the year I flew combat missions over Vietnam. I knew of many other combat veterans who had gone through the same experience: delayed stress syndrome, or post-traumatic stress disorder.

In any event, there seemed to be no other rational explanation. And because within hours I was back to my usual bouncy self, and because that weekend went by as if nothing unusual had happened, I had no reason to believe that I would experience another such attack again.

I was wrong.

One evening two weeks later, while driving home from work, once again I felt my stomach knot, just as it had knotted on my deck, and tears immediately began to pour down my cheeks. This time, though, there was nothing I could point to about the events of that day—nothing I had seen or heard in the media—that related directly to Vietnam. Over the next several weeks, the attacks continued—and at the most unpredictable times. I would be in my car, in church, even during staff meetings, and without warning an unexplainable sadness would well up inside my body, I would feel suddenly chilled, and tears would start spraying out of my eyes.

If you've never had this sort of experience yourself, it might be hard for you to imagine how unsettling it can be—not just to you but to the people around you, especially your family and coworkers, people who'd always considered you the Rock of Gibraltar. Now put yourself in the shoes of a hard-charging, super-cocky, ex-Top Gun pilot who had never experienced anything remotely resembling these episodes—not even in combat situations where his life was in imminent danger—and you might get a rough sense of how dumbfounded I was as these attacks continued.

What almost pushed me over the edge was that I couldn't come up with any logical or strategic way to respond to these attacks. Oh, I'd been out of control before. Fighter jets have a tendency to spin out of control, particularly when you're taking the plane through the kind of sharp, zigzag maneuvers you use in a dogfight or when you're training new pilots. In fact, one of the ways to determine a pilot's proficiency is to see how he handles himself and his airplane in these situations.

But the main thing they teach you in flight training—and they teach it to you relentlessly, over and over and over again—is what's called procedures and protocols: automatic, split-second responses to any of the myriad events that can occur while you're flying. And I considered it one of my greatest strengths that I always had my protocols down pat. Size up the situation. Get a plan. Execute.

That's been my approach to virtually every obstacle I've ever faced in my life. It's also how most people like me respond to crises. They don't think it over. They don't weigh the alternatives. They *act.*

This time, though, those patterned, cause-and-effect responses weren't working. I was pushing all the same buttons I'd always pushed whenever I was driven to the limits of my endurance, but I wasn't getting the results that I'd gotten when I was in a fighter jet. Instead of the "high" that comes when you have successfully tested your limits, I was experiencing panic. The "plane" wasn't responding. The spin was worsening.

I started to pray, although "negotiation" might be a better way of describing what I was actually doing. I was breaking down: fair enough. My overriding concern at the moment was timing: this was simply *not* a convenient time for this to be happening. I had a wife and three young children. I had a fledgling business with eight employees who'd put their future in my hands. So if it was indeed God's will that I go through a full-blown breakdown—and after a while this was exactly what I was beginning to think—what I wanted right now and what I was praying for was a little more time. Time to prepare. Time to get my affairs in order.

But not even prayer was able to stem either the frequency or the intensity of these attacks. And with each new attack, my panic intensified. My mind kept flashing to visions of the Jack Nicholson movie *One Flew over the Cuckoo's Nest.* I became more and more convinced that I was losing my mind.

As it happens, I *wasn't* losing my mind. But what was happening instead was something that can be no less frightening. I was beginning to discover who I was—who I really was, and who I wasn't.

I discovered that I was suffering from what I've come

to call the superman complex, a dangerously exaggerated need to achieve and an inflated idea of who I was (which has nothing to do with the man in the cape). And it was having a much greater impact on my life than I had realized—not just the occasional and brief emotional breakdowns that had led me to seek help.

My superman complex was affecting my personal and family relationships. It was affecting my work life and my relationships with my employees and coworkers. In dozens of different and very subtle ways, it was taking the joy out of my life and preventing me from finding fulfillment and satisfaction in everyday life.

As I became more and more aware of my superman complex and its effect on me, I began to realize that I had company—a lot of it. I began discovering others with the superman complex, people who were suffering the same consequences I was.

At first, I assumed that this was a business executive's ailment. But through speeches and conversations with others, I soon learned that anyone, of any age, race, gender, or occupation, can be a victim of the superman complex. In fact, people can be victimized by the superman complex in two different ways: they can have it themselves, which tends to rob them of the joy of living, or they can find themselves living with or working for someone with the superman complex, which can also make their lives miserable.

In 1988, I wrote an article for *Inc.* magazine describing my struggles with the superman complex, and I was inundated with letters from people who felt I was describing *them* or someone close to them. I began to realize just how much pain the superman complex was causing.

Over the years, with the help of my wife, my friends, my colleagues, and a wise and insightful therapist, I have gotten control of my superman complex. And I've learned a lot along the way, about what the superman complex really is, where it comes from, and most of all, how to deal with it.

I've written this book because I want to pass on what I've learned. I want to help people who have the superman complex—or are close to people who have it—to regain their balance, deepen their relationships, and find fulfillment in what they do.

I won't pretend to be a therapist or even a lay expert in the workings of the human mind, although I think I have picked up some useful information during my struggles. But I will tell you this: I know the truth of what you're about to read because I've *lived* it.

That's the truth I intend to share with you here. I'm confident that if you or someone you know has the superman complex, it will help you understand it better and deal with it more successfully.

Chapter One:
Addicted to Achievement

It was a long time before I realized achievement and success aren't the same thing.

Ever since I was a little boy, I'd dreamed of playing college football. That's why I went out for football in high school. I was a blocking back. Not as exciting as a running back, maybe, but I loved being out on the field and contributing to my team. More than anything, I wanted to do the same when I got to college, which, in my case, was Columbia College in New York City—where my dad had gone.

At college, I tried out as a freshman, even got a little playing time. Then, in my sophomore year, I went up to Columbia's preseason training camp for three weeks and was assigned to the last team, mostly playing tackling dummy for the first defense.

About halfway through, I was beaten to a pulp, and the coaches barely knew who I was. There wasn't much of a football future ahead of me, or so I thought. I was so disillusioned and downcast, I called my dad.

"Dad, this isn't what I bargained for," I told him. "I'm getting beaten up pretty good. More than that, I just don't see a place for myself. I'm not the fastest guy up here, but I am the smallest. All the other sophomores are getting more attention from the coaches than I am. I just don't think this is going to work. Maybe it's over."

"Well, why are you telling me this?" Dad asked.

"I guess I'm calling to get your advice on what I should do."

"I think you want my permission to quit. And I'm going to give it to you. Walk away, if that's what you want to do. And since you said you wanted advice, I'll give you a little of that too: you've been dreaming of playing football for Columbia for years, and, son, life has so few real dreams. I'd hate to see you walk away from your dream so easily."

He was right. Quitting would be an easy decision to make and a tough one to live with.

I decided not to give up, at least not yet. Instead, I notched up my effort and my focus. I worked on my tackling and I worked on my running. That made me feel I was doing something worthwhile.

When we came back from camp, I'd made the team—but at the end of the roster. Unfortunately, our first game is at Princeton. We can only take seventy-five players. That was the league limit. But the squad has seventy-eight. Three can't play and one of them is me.

I drove down to Princeton anyhow, to watch the game from the stands. And all my friends were there, even my kindergarten teacher. They knew I'd spent three and a half weeks at camp. They knew I was playing football for Columbia.

And everybody asked the same embarrassing questions: "Why aren't you on the field? I thought you were playing ball. I thought you made the team. I thought everyone was on the traveling squad." Once again I started to wonder whether this was the right thing for me. And I decided, sitting there in the rain, watching the game, that maybe Columbia football wasn't right for me.

I decided to quit right after the Princeton JV game on Monday, where I'd get my chance on the field. I said to myself, *How about I just go out this once and play my last football game for* me. For me. Not for any spectators—

probably wouldn't be any—not for my dad or my friends or even for the big coaches, who weren't likely to be there anyhow. For *me.* I decide that on every play I'm going to knock somebody down. Anybody gets in my territory, they're going down. I just love to hit people. Always have.

I also make a pact with myself on kickoff returns and punts: I'm going to catch those balls and I'm going to run with abandon. I'm going to run for *me* and I'm going to run for daylight. I'm going to have *fun,* and when the game is over, I'm going to quit. I'm going to end on the high that I always wanted, playing football for Columbia.

Then came the game. There were only a few people watching, just a couple of the junior coaches, but I played like a man possessed. Anybody crossed the field in front of me, they went down. Including the referee. I caught every punt and kick and I ran it. I didn't break anything for a touchdown, but I made all the yardage that was available to me. I tackled well, I tackled hard, I hustled, I did everything that I wanted to do. I made my statement. I was ready to quit.

Then I checked the game schedule. Next week was a home game against Harvard. Everybody on the team will dress, and everybody will be on the bench. Now that was homecoming weekend. I had a date, and she'd be at the game. A thought occurred to me: I'd be more likely to impress her if I'm wearing the uniform and on the team than if I'm sitting in the stands. I'll roll in the dirt a little at halftime—maybe I can fool her into thinking I've played. *Then* I can quit. After the game.

That week, at practice, the head coach pulls me over. First time he's ever noticed me. He hauls out a bag of balls. "Young man, you go down to the other end of the field here. I'm going to start punting these balls to you. You catch every ball I put into the air and you run it back to me. You understand?"

"Yes sir," I said. When the head coach is talking, I catch on quickly.

I run down there and he starts punting these balls to

me, one after another into the air—here, there, high, short, long. I catch 'em, I return 'em. By the time I returned one, there was another one in the air. He ran me ragged, until I could barely move. But I caught every ball that was catchable. Then, without a word to me, he was gone.

Then comes the Friday afternoon before the Harvard game. The coach calls out the first kickoff-receiving team—and I'm on it! He calls the first punt-receiving team, he calls my name! I'm incredulous and so is everyone else, even the other coaches. In one week I go from not making the traveling squad, about to quit, to being a starter on the first team.

I look back now and think: what if I had quit up at camp? What if my dad hadn't given me that advice at the perfect time? What if I'd quit because I didn't make the traveling squad? What if I hadn't played the JV game? What if, what if, what if? And that's solidified my belief in never quitting. Winston Churchill said it. He said never, never, never quit.

That year and the next two, I caught all the kicks and punts for Columbia. Became starter at right cornerback. Made an eighty-six-yard touchdown run against Princeton. Put Marv Hubbard from Colgate—later the Oakland Raiders' leading ground gainer—right out of the game with one tackle, 165 pounds against 240. Neutralized Calvin Hill from Yale. Ended up with five school records, one NCAA record, had a great career.

This is the good part of having the superman complex: being a fighter, being an achiever, playing hard for the team, proving—and pleasing—myself.

> *It's a fine thing to rise above pride, but you must have pride in order to do so.*
> —Georges Bernanos

I can't get no satisfaction

By the time I was out of college, I was pretty much addicted to achievement. Football success brought me satisfaction, but only temporary satisfaction. I needed more success, and more after that, again and again.

What's wrong with the desire to succeed? What's wrong with wanting to achieve? What's wrong with wanting to win? What's wrong with seeking recognition for your accomplishments?

There's the paradox of the superman complex. Nothing is wrong with any of those things. Nothing is wrong with ambition, determination, willingness to work, an ability to focus, an eagerness to confront challenges, a readiness to take command.

These are qualities we all admire, not only in others, but in ourselves. People with these qualities are anointed in the media. They drive great cars. They're asked for their opinions. Their children don't need scholarships to pay for college. They live—or they appear to live—rich and fulfilling lives. So what is this superman complex about anyhow?

It's about when we have too much—much too much—of some or all of these great qualities. It's about being too ambitious, too driven, too focused. It's about wanting, too intensely, to succeed, to win, to achieve.

It is too much of a good thing. *Much* too much. That's what the superman complex is, and when you have it—as I do—you can end up missing out on some of life's greatest satisfactions.

But when does a lot of a good thing become too much? What's the difference between ambition and monomania, between self-confidence and arrogance, between determination and utter sacrifice, between focus and obsession, between glowing when rewarded and being desperate to be recognized?

> *Ambition is the last infirmity of noble minds.*
> —J. M. Barrie

The six pillars of the superman complex

Looking at myself and at others I think have the superman complex, I see it is a combination of six different ways of acting, six different habits and inclinations that dominate our existence. I call these the six pillars of the superman complex:

1. The Renaissance man

Remember the original Renaissance man? That was Leonardo da Vinci, artist, sculptor, inventor, engineer and scientist. He could do anything and he could do it better than anyone else. Other people might have one talent or even a couple. Leonardo had 'em all.

Now if someone suggested to me that I think I'm another Leonardo, I'd laugh. But secretly, I'd have to admit the truth. People like me, who have superman complexes, think we can do just about anything we set our minds to, or we could have, if we'd just started early enough. We could have outpassed John Elway, outexec'ed Bill Gates, outdanced Fred Astaire, or outwritten Stephen King—if we'd chosen to. "I can do that," we say—and it doesn't matter what the task is.

A superman type, in his or her chosen field, can do anything, accomplish any goal, meet any deadline, solve any problem, overcome any obstacle. They are one-man bands, jacks-of-all-trades, sixty-minute men or women who can not only play but star at any position. Nothing and no one can stop them.

Of course, we don't usually proclaim our abilities. If

we did, others might think us wildly preposterous. But in our heart of hearts, that's what we really believe.

Why do we have such an inflated opinion of ourselves?

2. The know-it-all

We live in a world filled with experts, people whose knowledge is very deep but also very narrow. We call them lawyers. Or doctors. Or engineers. They know their fields very well, although they may not know much else.

People who have the superman complex, however, do not suffer from such limitations. They believe they are expert in every field of human endeavor. That doesn't mean they hold Ph.D.'s in everything. But they do have an opinion about everything, and they're right, or so they think. You'll never catch someone with the superman complex saying, "I don't have any opinion on that."

When we decide on a course of action, when we tell a subordinate how to do something, when we instruct our children on how they should live their lives, we're darn near infallible. That's because we've combined what actual knowledge we do have with our experiences, our observations of the world, and our instincts.

By the way, it isn't quite enough for us to be right. We also require that others admit we're right. It's fine if they admit it in advance, but when they admit it afterwards—after they've tried their way and fallen on their faces—that's especially delicious.

> *From a worldly point of view, there is no mistake so great as that of being always right.*
>
> —Samuel Butler

3. The glutton for punishment

In Greek mythology, Hercules was given twelve impossible labors to make up for his misdeeds, all of them well beyond the ability of any normal human being. They included not only killing a wide variety of terrible, man-eating beasts, but also cleaning up—in a single day—the thirty years of accumulated, um, waste left by thousands of cattle in the Augean stables.

What would we superman-complex types have said if we'd lived in mythological times and someone had given us twelve labors like that? We'd probably have said, "What? Only twelve? How about a thirteenth . . . or fourteenth . . . or fifteenth?" That's because we believe that no amount of work is too much for us, no matter how difficult it may be.

People with the superman complex are willing to sacrifice *anything* to get the job done, including not only our leisure time, but also our relationships with our families and even our physical and mental health. The job always comes first. We work 24/7/365.

"Work is my hobby," we tell ourselves and anyone else who asks. And we're actually proud of that. Long hours? Who cares? Overtime? Not a problem. Weekends? We volunteer. We suffer bravely. Why? To others, it seems like we're gluttons for punishment. But we know the simple truth: when all is said and done, we'd rather be working. Really. Why is work more important to us than anything else?

> *Nothing makes a man so selfish as work.*
>
> —George Bernard Shaw

4. The Lone Ranger

Of course, the Lone Ranger didn't exactly work alone. He had Tonto. (But it wasn't much of a relationship—*tonto* means "foolish" in Spanish.) But people with the superman complex don't need anyone at all. They can do it all by themselves. They *prefer* to do it all by themselves.

People like me—that is, people with the superman complex—feel that help is what's needed by the impoverished, or the disabled, or the totally decrepit—weaklings, that is. And we're anything but weaklings. So we have a problem asking for help or advice, because we'd be admitting weakness, and weakness is one thing people with superman complexes cannot tolerate in themselves. We don't have much use for it in others either, but more on that later.

Men are famous for not asking for directions when they're lost, but men with the superman complex take that much, much further. We're even reluctant to consult maps.

Why do we reject help and advice? Because we don't need any. We're Lone Rangers.

> *A man by himself is in bad company.*
> —Eric Hoffer

5. The puppet master

Ordinary folk drift with the tides. They go the way the wind blows. Not us superman-complex types. We are the captains of our ship. In fact, we try to be the captains of *all* the ships. Not only do we man the wheel, we set the sails, we read the compass, we batten down the hatches, we shanghai the crew, and we swab the decks.

In short, we control everything. Or we try to. Events. People. The competition. The marketplace. The weather.

Acts of God. Nothing escapes our eagle eyes. And nothing escapes our desire to c-o-n-t-r-o-l. We are loathe to let even a single minor detail slip through our fingers.

By the way, we don't limit our attempts to control to our work. Family situations also inspire the control-freak within us. Some superman-complex types even bring their passion for control to off-hours activities like golf or sailing. I know one superman-complex sufferer, for instance, who sailed up the East Coast with his wife. Just the two of them. By the time they got to their destination, Captain Bligh and Ms. Fletcher Christian were ready for the divorce courts.

Remember Michael Corleone (the Al Pacino character) in *The Godfather*? He controlled everything and everyone until, at long last, he was totally alone.

> *I have the same goal I've had ever since I was a girl. I want to rule the world.*
> —Madonna

6. The hall-of-famer

Some people are content to win once in a while. Some are satisfied to place second in a field of fifty. Some don't mind making three sales out of every four attempts. Some are content to climb the ladder of success rung by rung. Some believe the journey is more important than the destination.

Not people with superman complexes. We want to win all the time. With us, if we're not first, we're last. We're never content to climb up rung by rung when we can leapfrog. We'd be happy to ditch the journey altogether if we could get to our destination or reach our goal in an eyeblink.

This pillar of the superman complex is very much a

part of me—and of many successful people I know. We want all the prizes, honors, and rewards we can get our hands on. We want the promotions, the titles, the bonuses, the victories, and all the other goodies we deserve, and more. We want the respect, the admiration, even the awe that come with these rewards.

But we don't just want all these things. We need them. We need them because honors, rewards, praise, promotions, bonuses, and the approval of others reassure us that we're worthwhile. As I'll show you, people with the superman complex, and I include myself, need that extrinsic approval. And we need it again and again and again. Because it's this approval that allows us to believe we are the people we want to think we are.

So, what do I mean when I say I have the superman complex? I mean I habitually—although secretly—think that . . .

1. I can do anything (well, almost)
2. I'm always right
3. I can work nonstop
4. I don't need anyone
5. I'm in total control
6. My work is my life and my achievements give me my identity.

These are the pillars of my superman complex.

Of course, not everyone with the superman complex has all of these personality traits. Some of the people who have all of them don't have them to the extent that others do. Some people are more intensely superman types in one area, but less intensely a superman type in another.

The common denominator—the crux of the matter—is that the superman complex leads the people suffering from it to exaggerate their abilities, to believe in an image of themselves that, while it may have a kernel of truth, is a long way from reality. And that belief leads them to think, feel, and act in ways that don't fit.

In chapter 4, I'll cover in depth how you can recognize people who have the superman complex. I'll demonstrate how it shows up in their beliefs, their attitudes, and the way they behave, both in the workplace and in their personal lives.

often told people he couldn't be hurt by a punch in the stomach. And when he had a chance to tighten his muscles, that was usually true. But one day, someone slammed him in the gut without warning. His appendix burst and he died. Obviously, Houdini was a *glutton for punishment* and a *hall-of-famer* as well. He repeatedly ignored pain, which is one of the *glutton for punishment*'s chief characteristics, and he continually sought fame, which is what drives a *hall-of-famer.*

Ross Perot. The once-and-possibly-future U.S. presidential candidate has several times publicly demonstrated his superman complex is alive and well. He was not only the CEO of a major company, Electronic Data Systems, but he also influenced world events. You might remember when the Shah of Iran fell and the Ayatollah Khomeini became the country's leader. Several Perot employees were trapped in Iran. Perot, a true *Lone Ranger* in the superman complex sense, didn't turn to the government. He didn't waste much time appealing to Iran. Instead, he hired a soldier of fortune to do the job, the former Green Beret "Bull" Simons. He couldn't do the rescuing himself, but he could be the *puppet master* of the best soldier of fortune he could find. And Perot's puppet show had a happy ending. Simons successfully brought his people back to the United States. Around the same time, by the way, Jimmy Carter and the entire U.S. military establishment were failing to rescue over one hundred U.S. embassy employees.

> *Success has ruined many a man.*
> —Benjamin Franklin

Bill Gates. Mr. Microsoft. Mr. Monopoly. Now here's another fellow who seems to think he can control the world, at least the world of software and the Internet. Is that bad? Well, that's for history to judge. But would anyone lacking a superman complex willingly take on the multitude of competitors—and make the multitude of enemies—he has? I think not. His attempts to control his world are the modern version of Alexander the Great trying to control his—and a clear sign of a *puppet master* at work. Gates may have some other superman complex pillars as well. He shows signs of being a *Lone Ranger,* a *glutton for punishment* and a *hall-of-famer.* As far as he's concerned, limits don't apply—to him, anyhow.

Madonna. Yes, the singer, actress, author, social revolutionary, TV performer, and mother. With a résumé like that, you know she has to have a superman complex. And she's pretty much admitted it. "I'm anal retentive," she's written. "I'm a workaholic. I have insomnia. And I'm a control freak. That's why I'm not married. Who could stand me?" What we have here, in superman complex terms, is a confessed *glutton for punishment* and a *puppet master.* She may also be a *hall-of-famer,* someone who continually seeks honors and rewards. Many performers fit that description.

Bruce Jenner. Bruce Jenner won the decathlon at the 1976 Olympic Games, setting a new world record—and this after finishing tenth in 1972. Many superstar athletes have the superman complex, especially pillar #1, *Renaissance man,* and #3, *glutton for punishment.* Isn't that what it takes for a person to set out to prove he can run faster, jump longer, shot-put farther, jump higher, hurdle faster, vault higher, and throw the javelin farther than anyone else in the world?

> *How my achievements mock me!*
> —Shakespeare

Martha Stewart. It's hard to turn on your TV, day or night, without seeing Martha Stewart. She even owns her own TV production studios. This kind of behavior almost certainly indicates a *puppet master* at work. She also shows strong signs of being a *know-it-all.* The evidence? She's just started a new segment on her show, "Ask Martha." Why ask Martha? Because she knows, at least according to her.

Audie Murphy. Audie Murphy was probably best known as a second-string movie star, usually seen in westerns, mainly in the 1950s and 1960s. But Audie Murphy became famous for something else entirely. He was the most decorated American soldier of World War II, honored not just for one heroic act, but for many. Why does a man risk his life for his buddies again and again? Courage is certainly part of it. So is the willingness to sacrifice. Limits don't apply to him. But it's his superman complex that allows him to think he can succeed despite the odds. He's a *glutton for punishment*, and a *Lone Ranger*. He considers himself invulnerable. He believes that the rules of life don't apply to him. George Patton and Douglas MacArthur are two more military examples.

Donald Trump. At age twenty-eight, The Donald convinced New York City to build a convention center on the site of the defunct Penn Central railroad yards—on which he owned the option. Later, he built the Trump Tower—the name is significant—on Fifth Avenue. At various times Trump has also owned the Trump Shuttle airline, the New Jersey Generals of the United States Football

League (USFL), and casinos in Atlantic City, New Jersey. His big investments aren't in stocks or bonds or precious metals, but in the highest-profile projects he can find. He's a born *hall-of-famer*, and probably a *know-it-all, Lone Ranger*, and *puppet master* as well. Like many other men in his position, he wears his superman complex on his sleeve. And on the buildings he gives his name to.

> *I wasn't satisfied just to earn a good living. I was looking to make a statement.*
> —Donald Trump

Thomas Edison. In 1877—he was just barely thirty years old—Edison invented the phonograph. Two years later, it was the electric lightbulb. In 1882 he developed and installed in New York City the world's first large central electric power station. In 1888, it was the movie projector. In 1913, he demonstrated the first talking moving pictures. And he did all this, it's said, on four hours sleep a night, on a cot in his lab. Surely a superman complex was at work here. You can easily identify several of the pillars: *Renaissance man, glutton for punishment, know-it-all.* On the other hand, maybe Edison actually *was* superman.

Alan Shepard. Shepard was one of the first seven astronauts and the first American in space, riding the tiny Freedom 7 capsule 115 miles downrange on a fifteen-minute flight on May 5, 1961. But he was an overachiever long before that. He was one of the Navy's foremost carrier pilots, then one of its best test pilots. In 1971, Shepard commanded the Apollo 14 moon mission. When the radar failed just before touchdown, he made it clear to his copilot that he was ready to land no matter what—a perfect demonstration of his *Lone*

Ranger, know-it-all, glutton-for-punishment temperament. Fortunately, the radar came back on by itself. After his Mercury flight, Shepard was grounded because of an ear ailment, made chief of astronauts, and given an office. Like many people with a superman complex, Shepard had a temper and wasn't bashful about showing it. Every morning after he entered his office and closed the door, his secretary flipped a sign on it telling anyone who might come calling if his mood was good or bad.

Mary Kay Ash. Not everyone with a superman complex comes across as intimidating and unapproachable. A perfect example: Mary Kay Ash, the motherly and much-admired founder of Mary Kay Cosmetics, which now has annual sales of more than $1.5 billion. Being born to poverty has not stopped her from amassing a personal fortune of $320 million. Nor was she slowed by the glass ceiling that has stymied the careers of so many professional women. Like most of us with the superman complex, Mary Kay believed she could outwork and outthink practically anyone else.

Pete Rose. "Charlie Hustle," as he was called in his heyday—the hardest-charging major league infielder since Ty Cobb—believed with all of his heart that he could try harder than anyone else, which is a key characteristic of people with a superman complex. In his case, believing made it so. He had enough talent and determination to accomplish his goals. He was driven by several pillars of the superman complex: the *glutton for punishment*, the *Lone Ranger* and the *hall-of-famer*. Unfortunately, Rose's superman complex led him to think the rules didn't apply to him—the rules of gambling and the rules of professional baseball. He paid a terrible price for discovering he was just a human being, no more, no less. He was the ultimate *hall-of-famer*, whose superman complex has prevented him from ever being enshrined in the real thing.

> *Ultimately a hero is a man who would argue with the gods, and so awakens devils to contest his vision. The more a man can achieve, the more he may be certain that the devil will inhabit a part of his creation.*
> —Norman Mailer

Margaret Thatcher. It's the rare politician who doesn't suffer from the superman complex. After all, what sort of person actually thinks he or she is qualified to make decisions affecting the lives of millions? What kind of person has an ego large enough to aspire to lead a nation? Margaret Thatcher certainly did. Analytical, articulate, and ambitious, she drove herself and everyone around her unmercifully, and acted as though she were as infallible as the Pope. During her career, she displayed many superman qualities: *Renaissance man* (well, *woman*), *Lone Ranger, know-it-all, puppet master, hall-of-famer.*

Leona Helmsley. She's the wife of the late New York real estate tycoon, Harry Helmsley, and the overseer of the Helmsley Palace hotel. You may remember that she earned her fifteen minutes of fame—and some jail time as well—when she decided that "only the little people pay taxes," to use her words. Ms. Helmsley's superman complex is big enough to be seen from orbit. In word and deed, she has often proclaimed her superiority to most of the rest of humanity. She exhibits several superman complex traits—*puppet master, know-it-all, hall-of-famer*—and in her case, the combination is not attractive. Because she has the superman complex, she believes that rank has its privileges and that no one ranks higher than she does.

Robert Falcon Scott. In 1910 Scott set off on an Antarctic expedition, hoping to be the first person to reach the South Pole, a *hall-of-famer* goal if ever there was one. From McMurdo Sound, his party traveled 1842 miles, the longest polar sled journey ever made, clearly displaying his *glutton-for-punishment* qualities. Scott reached the South Pole on January 18, 1912, only to find that Norwegian explorer Roald Amundsen got there five weeks earlier. Scott and everyone else in his party died on the way back, a sacrifice to his superman complex, to his belief that normal human limits didn't apply to him.

> *Show me a hero and I will write you a tragedy.*
> —F. Scott Fitzgerald

Babe Didrikson Zaharias. The finest female athlete of the twentieth century, Babe Didrickson excelled at volleyball, tennis, baseball, basketball, and swimming in high school. Later, as a pro basketball player, she led her team to the national championship, often scoring thirty points or more per game. She was also a .400 hitter in the Dallas baseball league. She held American, Olympic, or world records in five track and field events. On one occasion, she won six gold medals and broke four world records in a single afternoon. After World War II, she became the most successful woman golfer of all time, winning seventeen straight tournaments. She continued to win even after coming down with the cancer that eventually killed her. She was a classic perfectionist, overachiever, workaholic, and control freak, displaying one of the most prominent superman complexes of her time.

Fifteen minutes of fame

I could go on forever listing famous people with demonstrable superman complexes. Consider these: Wayne Gretzky, Al Davis (president and general partner of the Oakland Raiders), Toscannini (the late and legendary orchestra conductor), Wilt Chamberlain (and I'm not talking about his basketball exploits here), Hillary Clinton, Vince Lombardi, Alfred Hitchcock, media tycoons Ted Turner and Rupert Murdoch, Michael Jordan, Chuck Yeager, John McEnroe, Jim Brown, Vladimir Horowitz, John D. Rockefeller, Picabo Street (how many more bust-ups is she willing to endure?), John Wayne—well, you get the idea. Among professional athletes, entertainers, and politicians, well, a superman complex practically comes with the territory.

What do all these people—and the dozens of others we describe in the book—have in common? All of them believe they can do more, faster and better than ordinary mortals—and their superman complex has driven them to prove it.

These people are all real. But the media has also given us all kinds of fictitious superman-complex types. From the movies, we have all those action movie heroes—Jean-Claude van Damme, Sylvester Stallone, Bruce Willis, and, of course, Arnold Schwarzenegger, whose muscle-building demonstrated a superman complex long before he became the Terminator (a robot with what I think is the strongest superman complex I've ever seen). TV has contributed its own corps of superman-complex types: Hercules, Young Hercules, Xena, the Teenage Mutant Ninja Turtles, the Power Rangers, and I'm sure I'm forgetting plenty of others.

If you have children who watch TV, they've been exposed. And, since kids tend to be copycats, a superman complex may be incubating within them at this very moment.

What does all of this add up to? All the famous people with superman complexes plus the media supermen-complex types? It tells us that this kind of behavior is commonplace in our society, completely normal by most standards, and quite often admired by all.

But let me emphasize that the superman complex is an affliction, and it isn't limited to well-known people. You can find it in homes and offices, in schools and government, in clubs and social gatherings, in prisons and college dorms. In fact, you can hardly escape it. If you can't find it in your own home or office, you can certainly find it right next door.

> *As a rule, all heroism is due to a lack of reflection.*
> —Ernest Renan

Chapter Three:

The Superman Next Door

According to the most recent counts, about 270 million people live in the United States. If only 1 percent of them have the superman complex, that's 2.7 million, or about four times the number of people who live within the city limits of San Francisco. Frankly, I wouldn't be surprised if the real total is ten or twenty times that many.

In my experience, people with a superman complex are everywhere. They're housewives and CEOs, shoe salesmen and chefs, nurses and pediatricians, plumbers and engineers, even surfers and punk rockers—any age, any race, either gender, any locale.

Maybe superman-complex concentrations do exist here and there. For example, I think occupations in which people put their lives at risk attract superman complex types: the military services, law enforcement, fire fighting. Same goes for people who control the fate of others: airline pilots, surgeons, and air traffic controllers.

I suspect you could also find an unusually high proportion of people with superman complexes in big cities or in dangerous neighborhoods. And I'll bet there are more people with a superman complex per one hundred residents in the United States than there are in, say, Tahiti or Finland or Costa Rica.

But these are just guesses. What I'm not guessing at is

that the superman complex is commonplace. I know because of the reaction I got when *Inc.* magazine published my autobiographical article, "The Superman Complex," in October 1988.

I was flooded with letters from total strangers—some of them people of national stature—thanking me for talking about a problem they'd been living with for years, or sharing their own superman complex stories with me, or telling me that the article had changed their lives because it forced them to face their problems.

Here are a few quotes from the letters, names omitted for privacy.

> *"Naval aviation was the great anesthetizer; re-enforcing the Golden Boy in all of us, while at the same time giving no room for 1) personal vulnerability and 2) the structuring of a support system. The results you so aptly summarized: dogmatism, less willingness to delegate, less understanding, more domineering, and the alienation from others—certainly I can relate these characteristics with my own personal experience."*

> *"I am a thirty-five-year-old who learned the hard way that I can never make it for long if I try to do it myself. Thank you for the reminder. I am blessed with a wonderful staff because I make a concerted effort to let them know that I am less than perfect. And, that I need them if we are going to get the job done."*

> *"I am passing your article on to a forty-six-year-old business owner who is ranting and raving at his people and drinking too much. I know he will read it and understand."*

> *"I am writing to simply thank you for your willingness to bare your heart and soul so that the rest*

of us might be reminded that we too are only human."

"There were a number of parallels in the experience you had and the things that happened to me; and I will draw on your experience to try to correct the problems I had."

"The 'I am in control' syndrome and the security that it represents can come crumbling down if we really look at our world. Fortunately for some of us, that surrendering process can lead to someone greater to rely upon."

Since writing the article, I've often spoken about the superman complex to business groups and other audiences. The reaction is always the same. Invariably, people come up to me afterwards to share their feelings, to tell their superman-complex stories, or to ask for advice about their spouses or bosses or someone else in their lives.

I've discovered that the superman complex doesn't always look the same, or strike with the same intensity. It can take on a number of different guises, depending on the person and the circumstances. It can be mild or severe.

To give you an idea of what I mean, and to help you spot the superman complex in action, either in yourself or in others, I talked to a few people I believe suffer from it. I promised not to reveal their actual names in the book, so they were remarkably frank with me.

As you read their comments, see if you can spot the superman-complex characteristics. Here they are again: 1) Renaissance man, 2) know-it-all, 3) glutton for punishment, 4) Lone Ranger, 5) puppet master, and 6) hall-of-famer.

1. The supermom

> *If you bungle raising your children, I don't think whatever else you do well matters very much.*
>
> —Jacqueline Kennedy Onassis

Celia Strickland is a thirty-something mom, with a pediatrician husband and two young boys, eight and four. She was a successful TV writer before she got married, but gave up her career to raise her children.

You've said you see yourself as a superman. Tell me how.

I mentioned this to my friends and said that I didn't quite see why being a particularly driven parent was such a bad thing. They all began laughing, and said, "Well, there are people who are reasonable about it." I kind of act as though every single day I have to attend to my children's needs in every single way.

Are they easy kids or are they difficult?

I feel as though they are always on the verge of going out of control, but I nip it in the bud. I've always felt that people can control almost everything in their life. I've gotten angry at my eight-year-old for passing gas because I think he can control that. My husband doesn't agree. He says that I am overly controlling and a perfectionist, and he's very easygoing, very warm.

How do you try to control your kids and what does your husband say about that?

I remember getting furious with my four-year-old when he was three and he got sick of trying to learn how to read, and I walked out of the room on him, and my husband happened to be home, and he said, "You know, this is the sort of thing that makes me feel like calling social welfare on you. You've tied all your pride up with his achievements, and that's not a good thing."

How do you react when your husband criticizes the way you're treating the kids?

If we are alone, I will get very cold and angry, and try to control my husband trying to tell me I'm being controlling, but if we are with the children, I act very receptive to what he is saying. I want my children always to be the first and the best, and I think all mothers feel that way. But I guess my problem is that I *really* feel that way. I couldn't bear to think any other baby could walk at a younger age than my son, or do as well at school.

What do you say when your eight-year-old brings home papers that have mistakes on them?

I don't think he'd show me any like that. Everything that he brings home is perfect. But I have often wondered if he crumples things up and puts them in the garbage can.

How would you like your kids to turn out?

I found a book written by Franklin Roosevelt's mother because I thought, who do I want my children to be like? She reminded me of myself. She was a very controlling mother, and a very loving mother. She wrote this book on how she raised little Franklin, and it was wonderful, you know, because all the things that I will get criticized for by other people, she did with abundance.

So that's your ambition for your child, to be another Franklin Roosevelt?

Yeah, I'd love that.

Are you controlling in other aspects of your life?

Yes, yes, I would say so. I am president of the Mother's Society in Cincinnati, for example, and every year I say that's enough, I am not going to continue being president, but every year, I can't bear the thought that someone else's philosophy would reign over mine.

They wouldn't do as good a job?

Yes. And I tend to feel sorry for people who disagree with me—it's a terrible shame that God didn't grant them more intelligence. At the same time, I know that's wrong, but that's only when my intellectual side catches up, you know, and then I will try to apologize to someone for being hostile or demeaning or cold.

Does Celia Strickland have a superman complex? Well, what do *you* think? She's certainly a classic puppet-master—a control freak. She also shows clear signs of being a hall-of-famer, once removed. The recognition she seeks is not for herself, but for her children. She'll ride high on their accomplishments.

2. The CEO

> *Executives are like joggers. If you stop a jogger, he goes on running on the spot. If you drag an executive away from his business, he goes on running on the spot, pawing the ground, talking business.*
>
> —Jean Baudrillard

For three years, Frank Hogan, fifty-six, has been CEO of a communications equipment company that last year grossed $5.6 billion. He has three children, two by his first wife and one—a two-year-old—by his second wife, whom he married just before his promotion. Frank had a heart attack six years ago, but has fully recovered. He now jogs ten miles a day, regardless of the weather.

What makes a good CEO in your opinion?

Well, some of it's temperament, of course. But to my mind, there's no substitute for experience and knowledge. It's impossible to have enough of either. You gotta know finances, you gotta know marketing, you gotta know production, you gotta know how to plan, how to hire, how to fire, how to say yes, how to say no. You gotta be able to outthink the competition. You gotta have imagination. You gotta know the industry. You gotta know about government relations, about community relations, about public relations. You gotta be an economist, a psychologist; hell, it wouldn't hurt if you were every kind of "ologist" there is, including proctologist.

Do you fit the description?

Oh yeah, one other thing: you gotta have self-confidence. And I do. I know I can do the job. To be perfectly frank, I don't think anyone could do it better than I can. Yeah, I fit the description. I'd better fit the description.

What's your single-best CEO quality?

I'm a terrific decision-maker. Give me the facts, give me the circumstances and out comes a decision—nine times in ten, the right decision. That's the way my brain works.

Ever change your mind?

Well, I make mistakes, of course. Gotta say that, you know, even if I don't actually think it's true.

Were you brought up to be a CEO?

Hah! Maybe my mother thinks so. No, I was a normal kid. Well, I was an achiever. You know, class president. Editor of the paper. Basketball. National Honor Society. Phi Beta Kappa at Princeton. Mensa. I was brought up to achieve. My father expected me to be the best at anything I did. He demanded it.

Do you have a talented staff to help you?

I guess it's okay. Sometimes it seems I have to make a choice between people who are loyal and people who are talented. It's hard to find both in the same package, I don't know why. Just when I think I've got myself a good president or VP of marketing, he leaves for some other job. One way or another, I have to watch 'em like hawks. I can't let them make big decisions without checking on them. If I did, they'd sink us. I can't trust 'em either. Not completely. They don't always tell me the truth, they tell me what they think I want to hear.

Is being CEO a lonely job?

Well, there's a steady stream of people in and out of my office, lotta meetings, conferences, social functions, and all that. But yeah, in a way it's lonely. I mean, in the end, who can I ask? Oh sure, I hear from consultants and subordinates. The board has its opinions. But it's really all on me. Everything starts in my office and it ends here too.

That's a heavy responsibility.

Yeah, maybe. But I'm comfortable with it. I know what to do with it.

You're never troubled by self-doubt?

Self-doubt is a waste of time. It weakens you. It makes you cautious and that leads to mistakes. I don't have time for it. I think it's an indulgence, you know, like a bad habit.

So you don't allow yourself this indulgence?

Absolutely not.

How does your family fit into this picture?

My wife and I have a division of labor. I take care of the business, she takes care of the house. That works out perfectly. Keeps my mind clear for what matters. Of course, we've worked out all the details—the budget, scheduling her time at the gym, determining the housekeeper's hours. She just makes sure things go according to plan.

Does Frank Hogan have a superman complex? I'd say he has a classic case. He sees himself as a Renaissance man and a know-it-all. But he's also a glutton for punishment and a Lone Ranger. He treats his wife as an employee, which makes him a puppet master. He's probably a hall-of-famer as well, although he seems satisfied, at the moment, with just being CEO of one of the Fortune 100 largest companies in America.

Does this man sound like anyone you know? Like you . . . or your spouse . . . or your boss? If so, watch out. There's a superman in the house.

3. The airline pilot

John Linkladder, fifty-four, has been an airline pilot for nineteen years and a captain for thirteen. He commands a Boeing 747 and usually flies New York to Paris or Rome. He married a flight attendant ten years ago and has a seven-year-old son.

What do you like best about your job?

Oh, I like knowing that I'm responsible for the lives of two or three hundred people, that they're depending on my skills and my experience to get where they're going.

Do you ever feel the burden of that responsibility?

Well, I take my job seriously of course. But I don't have any trouble sleeping nights, if that's what you mean. I can handle it.

Things ever go wrong up there?

(laughs) Oh yeah. Couple of near misses. Slid off a runway at Heathrow once. Had an engine die over the Atlantic. Lost some parts in flight. Then there were the usual passenger heart attacks and a couple of premature births. You know, little stuff like that.

Little stuff?

If you live to tell about it, it's little stuff.

Have you ever been scared?

Not during. But afterwards, yes. When I have an in-flight problem, I'm just too focused on solving it to worry. Besides, I have a pretty high degree of self-confidence. I've been flying all my life, you know. I've flown everything you can think of, from hang gliders to single-engine private planes, from jet fighters to bombers and tankers, from DC-3s to 767s. I've even done some helicopter time. There's nothing I can't fly.

What do you do when you're not on the job?

I have a workshop in my basement. I make Windsor chairs, highboys, and other antique furniture reproductions. Some of my work is in the Smithsonian. I also collect stamps. I concentrate on European issues.

Does your family mind that you travel so much?

We have an understanding about that. My wife is an ex-flight attendant. She knows what it's like.

Does John have a superman complex? Well, he's comfortable playing God and he seems convinced he's invulnerable. Those are two pretty good indicators. Fortunately, both for his passengers and for himself, he's a very capable pilot.

He fits the profile in other ways as well. He's clearly a Renaissance man—broad flying experience, maker of museum-quality furniture reproductions, major league stamp collector. He's also a Lone Ranger. Making furniture and collecting stamps are not exactly family entertainment.

Lots of pilots have a superman complex, and I'm a good example. When you're constantly risking your life and the lives of others, it's almost a necessity. That works out okay as long as your capabilities match your confidence. When you overreach yourself, however, the result can be deadly.

4. The supernurse

Judy Grant, who is in her late thirties, has been a nurse all of her working life. She currently runs a very active hotline for physicians and nurses dealing with serious burn cases. She has three children, a nineteen-year-old daughter who is deaf (but a very successful college student), a sixteen-year-old son who has cancer (but is doing well) and a thirteen-year-old daughter. Judy herself had a double mastectomy a few years ago, at almost the same time she learned her son had cancer. She's also recovered from a spinal cord injury and broken bones received from a fall down a flight of stairs. She is married.

You've had some problems in life.

Yeah, but I consider it a fortunate life. Every bit of it has offered many blessings, many reminders that I am where I am supposed to be.

You sound like a very strong person.

Yeah, maybe it's the stubbornness in me, but I can't think of anything that would break me down. When I was seventeen, I moved out on my own, and in order to afford to be out on my own, I worked three jobs and went to school full time. I've rarely had fewer than three jobs since then.

How long have you been a nurse?

About twenty-five years. I started out as an oncology nurse, dealing with cancer patients. It was back in the days when we lost everybody. So it was pretty scary when my own son got it.

Are you doing anything now besides running the hotline and taking care of your son?

For the first time in my life, no. Usually I have at least two other jobs. Also, I usually run a church organization that gets kids off the street on graduation night, and I do the fund-raising. But I'm in a lull at the moment.

That must be a relief.

Actually, I feel as though I'm letting myself down. I really have to start getting busy soon.

Are your children like you?

My daughter is identical. Even though she's hearing-impaired, she was an honor student in high school, by lip-reading. Now she's in college, with three majors—pre-law, international studies, and English; she's in two honor sororities and one fraternity; she led the program in December to see the Pope; and she travels the country for the college. Pretty good for a girl who's had eleven surgeries.

How about your husband?

Last year, he was downsized by his company, and so he took six months off, and you know, played around with the boats and stuff. Now he's back working full-time work again.

Did it bother you to see him just tinkering?

Yeah. I just have to sit back and come to the discovery that my husband has other priorities.

What will you do when the children are grown?

I'm afraid I'll start climbing the ladder again—afraid because I don't know when to stop. Everything I achieve makes me want to achieve more. If that wasn't enough, that wasn't fulfilling, maybe I could try another mile, you know, like when I used to jog long distance. I had stress fractures all over, and was still jogging ten to fifteen miles, and was still going to do that triathlon, you know?

Clearly, Judy Grant has a superman complex. She is a Renaissance woman—she nurses, she runs a business, she cares for her own seriously ill children, she fund-raises, she runs an organization. She's a glutton for punishment, a major-league workaholic. And if you look closely, you can see other superman complex characteristics as well—a bit of the Lone Ranger, some puppet master, and a dash of hall-of-famer. Nothing short of a well-aimed bazooka shell can stop her from what she sets out to do, which far exceeds the abilities of ordinary mortals.

5. The surgeon

> *Surgeons must be very careful,*
> *When they take the knife!,*
> *Underneath their fine incisions,*
> *Stirs the Culprit—Life!*
> —Emily Dickinson

Harold Weaver, forty-five, is a general surgeon at a small New England hospital about forty miles from Boston. He's married and has two teenage girls. Every weekday morning (except Wednesday, when he usually golfs with other physicians, at least in season), he commands the hospital's Operating Room #1. There, he removes gall-bladders, replaces hips, does hysterectomies, takes out appendices. Patients come to him from a hundred-mile radius, despite his proximity to Boston, home to several of America's best hospitals and many of its finest doctors. He is widely known, well respected, and quite rich.

What's it like when you're performing an operation?

When I'm in the operating room, I'm the king, the captain of the ship. What I say goes. And the other medical personnel know they'd better snap to. I demand quick obedience because I bear the ultimate responsibility for the life of the patient on the operating table. All I ask is that they follow procedure.

It's pretty different when you're not on the job though, right?

At home? Well, it's kind of the same way. I mean, I'm responsible for my family, aren't I? Their health, their well-being. And of course I handle the money, except for my wife's household account and the girls' allowances. But I don't want you to think I ignore what my wife says or thinks. I don't. I factor it into every decision. But how can a family have two bosses?

To what do you attribute your success?

It's not just one thing. Part of it is my work capacity. I've never met a surgeon who was faster than I am. Versatility is important too. Which I am. And endurance. Surgery is hard work. But I'm kind of like the Energizer Bunny. I can just keep going and going and going.

What happens when you reach your limit?

(laughs) Hasn't happened yet.

How do you relax?

(laughs again) My work is my hobby.

No, seriously.

I play golf on Wednesday. Of course, that's with other physicians. Also, I go to a lot of medical conferences. I was in Miami three weeks ago. Dallas next month.

Do you feel you're living a fulfilling life?

I think I have all the good things life has to offer—all the material stuff I mean, and a beautiful family, and privileges at three excellent hospitals. I've been Physician of the Year four times. And I have a file full of letters from patients thanking me, some of them for saving their lives. The respect of my colleagues. So, yes, you could say fulfilling.

What does the future hold for you?

Within the next five years, I expect to become president of the state medical association and maybe even a board member of the American Medical Association. Then, when the hospital chief of staff retires, I would be the obvious candidate to replace him. I've already had some feelers.

Does Dr. Weaver have a superman complex? It certainly seems that way. His work is his life. He believes he has abilities beyond those of ordinary mortals. He gets fulfillment largely from external sources. With that cluster of symptoms, it would be a miracle if he didn't have the disease itself.

At least in his own mind, Dr. Weaver is a Renaissance man, a know-it-all, a Lone Ranger and a hall-of-famer. If he sounds like a doctor you know, don't be surprised. I think the field of medicine tends to attract people with a superman complex. It's enormously demanding both physically and intellectually, it gives you the power of life and death, it offers all kinds of opportunities for respect and even adulation, and there's a big material payoff. All of this reinforces and encourages superman behavior.

6. The athlete

> *Is it normal to wake up in the morning in a sweat because you can't wait to beat another human's guts out?*
> —Joe Kapp

Gerald Jonas, twenty-nine, has been a starting NFL linebacker for six years, All-Pro for three of them, and before that he was an All-American at a Big Ten school. He's married and has two young children. During his NFL career, he has never missed a single game and he's led his team in tackles every year he's played. He'll be a free agent next year and expects several teams to compete to pay him millions of dollars a year for at least four years for his services.

You've always played on a winning team, haven't you?
That's true—high school, college, and the pros. Never had a losing season, got some championship rings.

Do you think the teams would have won without you?
Well, victories are a team effort of course, but every player likes to think he makes a crucial contribution. I do have a pretty big collection of game balls, though. You don't get game balls by watching on the sidelines, you know.

What would you say makes you so good at your job?
I guess mainly total commitment. When I'm out there,

nothing—and I do mean nothing—can distract me.

Not even pain?

Especially not pain. There's plenty of time to feel pain after the game.

You've been injured?

I play injured all the time. Lots of guys do. It's part of the game. I've had a dislocated shoulder, several broken fingers, cracked ribs, sprained knees and ankles. But nothing's going to stop me short of a tank.

How does your wife feel about that?

I guess Laura worries about me, but hell, she knew who I was when we got married. Football isn't croquet. You gotta put yourself on the line. She knew that. She knew the game comes first with me.

What do you think makes a player an All-Pro?

Three things: you gotta be able to read the offense, you gotta be fast, and you gotta hit like a son-of-a-gun. Or, if you look at it another way, desire, focus, and ability.

And you have all that?

Well, Coach thinks so. The opposing team usually thinks so. The running backs who try to get past me think so. (laughs)

How did you get so good?

There's nothing secret about it. I just work harder than anyone else. I spend more time in the weight room than anyone else. I watch more game videos than anyone else. When I walk out there, I'm the most prepared guy on the field.

But you're not one of the team captains.

That's just a popularity contest. I don't care about that. I'll let other people be the nice guy. I'll be the son-of-a-gun who nails the guy with the ball.

How long do you plan to play?

You mean when am I going to retire? Hell, they're going to have to shoot me.

Obviously, Jonas belongs in the superman-complex category, subtype *athleticus invulnerabilis*. He's a glutton for punishment. What else could you call a man whose profession is colliding with fast-moving running backs trying to trample him? What else could you call a man who's proud of his injuries and his pain?

He's also a Lone Ranger. Some football players see themselves as leaders or at least team players. But despite the obligatory "team player" lip service, I think Jonas genuinely believes he can do it all.

Someday, of course, Jonas will discover that he is no longer superman. He'll have to pack up his cleats and head for the broadcast booth. Or maybe he'll take up coaching, where his superman complex can operate in a different but equally superhuman way.

For now, however, he's superman on the football field, and not the only one either. Professional sports are crowded with people whose superman complex is totally in charge of their lives, and with people who eventually find out that their bones are as breakable as anyone else's, that they eventually lose a step and get beaten by someone else with a superman complex, only younger.

7. The movie producer

> *The human tendency to regard little things as important has produced very many great things.*
> —G. C. Lichtenberg

Mike Cornish, fifty-six, has been making TV documentary and corporate films for nearly thirty years. He's won all the awards his industry has to offer, second only to Ken Burns. He has a grown daughter and he's on his third marriage, to a woman about half his age.

What's the hardest thing about producing movies?

The details. Moviemaking, even documentaries, involves millions of details—choosing the location, casting the talent, principal photography, sound recording, the music track. And each of them involves a thousand more details. And I'm not including the getting-money part or the distribution part.

So you're a juggler?

(laughs) Yeah, that's right. Or maybe more like a puppet master. I gotta make sure the caterer is there on time, I gotta get the right equipment delivered to the right place, I gotta see that the crew is awake and fed and on the set.

But you enjoy doing it, right?

Suits me just fine, keeping track of everything, making sure nothing goes wrong, making sure everything goes right and everyone does his job. I like being in control and I'm damn good at it. Ask anybody. I'm proud to say I never miss a trick.

What happens if something goes wrong?

Then I fix it. That's my job. And there's not much I can't fix.

Do people like working with you?

Well, I hope they do, sometimes they do. Sometimes they don't. I'm pretty demanding. You can't tolerate mistakes in this business. One small mistake can cost ten thousand dollars. I don't think producers are well liked in general, but that's not important. We can't be nice guys and do our jobs right.

Does that bother you?

Honestly, I don't think about it. I think about keeping to the budget, getting the project done, getting it distributed, maybe winning an award or two.

What do you do in your leisure time?

(prolonged laughter)

Does Mike Cornish have a superman complex? Well, he has many of the characteristics. He craves being in control. He's confident that he can do anything. His work is his life. His main goal in life is achievement. He's a kind of puppet master, Lone Ranger, glutton for punishment, hall-of-famer.

None of these qualities is bad—in moderation. It's good to feel in control. It's good to have confidence in yourself. It's good to work for achievement. But for someone with a superman complex, there's no such thing as moderation. Such people are driven by these feelings, even consumed by them.

As you've been reading these case histories, I'll bet you've been thinking of yourself . . . or your spouse . . . or your boss. How can you spot a superman complex? Read on.

Chapter Four:

How to Recognize the Superman Complex

When you're a combat pilot, you're trained to control everything you possibly can. But my fellow pilots and I believed that eventually, every one of us would have our time "in the box." That's the time when everything conspires against you. On any given night or any given afternoon, one mistake piles up on another. And another. Until the odds against you are almost insurmountable.

The night "in the box"

> *No passion so effectually robs the mind of all its powers of acting and reasoning as fear.*
>
> —Edmund Burke

It started innocently, with what seemed like a completely rational decision. I said to myself, "I'm not going to have any problems tonight, so I don't have to waste time hooking up to the tanker and topping off my gas tanks."

And then I made a second decision. "Well, the weather isn't as good as it should be, but it's not as bad as it could be either, so even with minimal gas, I'll be okay. After all, I'm probably not going to have an emergency. I'll keep going."

Then comes a third decision, quite sensible actually if you forget about the first two. "I'm in-country now, I might as well go on to the target. I didn't get a good hit last time and I want one more chance at it. That'll run down the gas a little, but I should be able to get back without too much trouble."

They say that when it's your turn in the box, you nail yourself in with your own poor decisions, or bad rationalizations, one after the other, until you're completely enclosed. Well, I didn't know it at the time, but that's what I was doing to myself.

By now, I was flying over the beach with my wingman, me in the lead, into Vietnam. I must have made a small navigational error, because after a few minutes, I realized that I'd led my wingman over a place called Vinhsanh, the home of the North Vietnamese gunnery school. When unlucky American planes entered that airspace, the students started practicing—throwing up as much lead as they could, hoping to knock us out of the sky.

Suddenly, every cockpit radar warning device started sounding simultaneously. We were in deep trouble. Moments later, the skies were filled with exploding missiles on our right, on our left—everywhere. I was twisting and turning through the air, gritting my teeth against the possibility of being hit. Somehow, we managed to come out unscathed, both of us. But I was positively vibrating from the massive adrenaline dump.

We dropped our bombs on the nearest target and headed back to the ship—still feeling disjointed and agitated from the adrenaline. Now I began to think of my next big task: landing my fighter on the carrier at night, in stormy weather and rough seas. I started feeling apprehensive again.

When I began to psych myself up for the last forty-five

seconds before touchdown, I realized my movements were ragged. The adrenaline was still pumping through my veins. I was agitated, and the Landing Signal Officer could hear it in my voice. He's the guy on the ship who literally "talked you through" your final approach.

I didn't make the very smooth, very small, very controlled and accurate corrections necessary for landing. Mine were big, rough—and wrong. My flight path wasn't safe. I was coming down too fast. I hit the deck hard, my landing gear bounced, my hook skipped over the wires, and I was airborne again. That's called a bolter. Now the LSO knew I might be a problem that night.

I flew back up, came back around to set up again. Then, another bolter. Number two.

My radio came on. "Hello, Carey, this is the captain. Are you there?"

"Yes, Captain. I'm here."

"Pretty rough out there tonight, huh?"

"Captain, you have no idea—shot at, storms, pitching deck . . ."

"I know, I know," he said, "but I need to tell you something. Do you know how much it costs to steam a carrier into the wind?"

"No, sir."

"Sixty thousand dollars a minute."

"I see."

"Do you know you're the only airplane that hasn't landed yet?"

"No sir, I didn't realize that."

"Do you think you might grace us with a landing on the next time around?"

"Yes, sir, I'll try."

A little bit of levity to break the ice—but would it? I came back around, set up aft, a little rough, but making good corrections. I got in close, then the deck flattened out on me, I added too much power—again!—landed long—again!—and bounced right back up into the air. Again! Bolter number three. By then, I was below one thousand pounds of gas. I've seen cigarette lighters that could hold more than that.

I went around again and headed back up to set up, determined to do it right this time, to land short enough to give my tailhook a shot at all the deck wires. And I did land short, but I landed hard and my nose fell and kicked up the hook, the hook failed to catch any wires and I was airborne again! Bolter number four.

The captain launched a tanker to refuel me. On the radio, another pilot was teasing me. "Wouldn't you like to come back down and land and have something nice to eat tonight, and maybe a cocktail?"

By the time I got gassed up, it was 2:30 A.M. I dropped back down for pass number five. I was really rattled by then. I come in to land, and, boom, up I go again, fifth bolter. I'm beginning to wonder what the record is.

The captain comes on the radio. "Carey, this is the captain."

"Yeah, captain, I recognize your voice."

"Carey, we all know what's going on out there with you tonight, but I want you to know I've just told the crew to man the forward guns and if you don't land on the next pass I've ordered them to shoot your ass down as you go by. You got that Carey?"

"Yes, Captain, I've got it."

And I came back around that pass and I landed. I brought it in, I planted it, I pulled back on the stick and just made that hook catch those wires. Later, I found out that other pilots had been watching me for the past twenty minutes on the ship's closed-circuit TV system, eating popcorn, cheering, laughing, jeering—and grading every one of my landing attempts and posting them on a chart for everyone to see.

However I might have rationalized it—then, or even now—the fact is that I got in trouble that night by blindly relying on the invulnerability I imagined I had. And that almost cost me my life. Now landing an airplane on an aircraft carrier is not exactly an everyday event, I admit, but people with a superman complex like me can get themselves into trouble in some pretty ordinary circumstances, if they convince themselves they're greater than they really are.

Does someone in your life have the superman complex?

Do you—or does your spouse, your boss, or your parent—suffer from a superman complex? Maybe you've felt a sense of recognition in what you've read so far, but you're not sure. You may also suspect you're working with someone who has the superman complex, or married to someone who does.

How can you be sure, one way or the other?

To answer that question for yourself or for someone who plays a major role in your life, we're going to look at how people view themselves and how they behave. The signs and symptoms of the superman complex are unmistakable. That goes for the people in your private life and the people in your work life. We'll look at both.

A word of caution

Every human being has some talents, capabilities, and knowledge. Every human being wants to achieve something, some more than others. If you are ambitious, focused, energetic, hardworking, and dedicated, you do not necessarily have a superman complex. As you'll see, it's when these qualities and others like them swell up to occupy your very being that you have a superman complex. It's when these values become so important to you that other values hardly matter at all.

Also bear in mind that some superman complexes are more exaggerated than others. On a scale of one to ten, Nero's superman complex, for instance, was a solid ten.

He genuinely believed he was a god. He was so far above normal human concerns that he fiddled while Rome burned, or so it's said. Now consider Bruce Jenner. Maybe he was driven by a superman complex, but he had a pretty realistic view of his true abilities. He set records. He won the gold medal. Surely he is no more than a five, and maybe a lot less.

One more caution: you (or the person you're judging) probably won't fit the superman-complex description in every respect. You'll lack some symptoms entirely, or they'll be so mild they won't matter. Or, your superman complex might be limited to a few symptoms, but still intense enough to affect your life and the lives of those around you.

The six pillars

As we've seen, people with the superman complex have one or more of six basic characteristics—the six pillars. But it may not be easy to see them, since they may be swathed in geniality, power, silence, or a number of other superficial disguises.

How, then, can you spot the underlying symptoms? How can you tell if the person you're living with—or working with—is truly afflicted with the superman complex? How can you tell if you have the superman complex? And how can you be sure of your diagnosis?

Well, you're about to get a short course in the signs and symptoms of the superman complex, as it shows up at work and in nonwork situations, based on my observations of myself and others like me. You're going to be able to spot each of the six pillars of the superman complex even if the person doesn't realize he has them. Even if the person is you.

Keep in mind, as you read these signs and symptoms, that what I've laid out here is the superman complex at its absolute worst. It sounds very negative, and indeed, it can be very negative. More often than not, however, people with the superman complex will have many redeeming qualities. Their superman complexes won't always be in control. And their superman-complex behavior may be brief and mild, even benign. But I suspect you'll also know people who perfectly match these worst-case scenarios.

1. The Renaissance Man

How to spot him (or her) at home

- He's a jack-of-all trades, an electrician, a plumber, a carpenter, an auto mechanic, a chef, a tour navigator, and everything else anyone might need.

- There's nothing he can't do, and better than anyone else around—at least in his opinion. He's truly puzzled when others don't recognize his talents.

How to spot him (or her) at work

- He's the model for the original one-man band. He can give speeches, he can manage, he can analyze, he can sell, he can troubleshoot, he can give advice.

- He knows how to do your job, in fact, anyone's job better than they do. He can type better than his secretary, figure finances better than the chief financial officer, relate to the press better than the public relations guy, design products better than the engineering staff, and write better ads than the ad agency.

- He tends to hog responsibility, development of new projects, the big decisions, and other activities that could help subordinates develop and grow, because he wants things done right and is convinced that he can do them right better than anyone else.

- He has an inflated opinion of himself and expects others to agree.

2. The Know-it-All

> *We should take care not to make the intellect our god; it has, of course, powerful muscles, but no personality.*
> —Albert Einstein

How to spot him (or her) at home

- He knows all the answers in *Jeopardy*. He's a scholar in every homework subject. He knows the right way to do everything—his way, not yours.

- He can spot others' mistakes at a glance, and from a great distance. He enjoys proving his point.

- He feels sorry for the rest of humanity, which unfortunately is not as knowledgeable as he is. He tries not to let others know he thinks they're stupid or misinformed.

- His word is final.

How to spot him (or her) at work

- He's right more often than anyone else. When he says something, when he offers an opinion, listen up. Because he's right.

- His judgment is better, his knowledge is greater, and his instincts are truer than anyone else's—he believes.

- He is unbearably certain. He hates it when others waste his time by disagreeing with him. He isn't interested in other people's opinions, because they're rarely right (if they differ with him).

- His subordinates are gun-shy about expressing their opinions, because he's likely to dismiss them with contempt. They're likely to feel enormous self-doubt.

- His subordinates also tend not to tell him the truth, especially if it contradicts his expectations, because they have often seen him kill the messenger.

- He dominates conversations and meetings. He doesn't hesitate to interrupt others, because he grasps their ideas almost before he hears them and he knows whatever he says is more valuable than whatever anyone else might be saying.

- Others may fumble or stumble, others may not get it, others may have to figure it out first—not him. He understands complicated matters instinctively. He catches on so quickly he even surprises himself.

- He holds vast amounts of information in his head.

- He never gets confused, except when someone else doesn't explain something clearly.

3. The Glutton for Punishment

How to spot him (or her) at home

- He isn't home much—he's working late, or off on a business trip, or off to the office before anyone else is awake.

- When he is home, no one sees him much. He's in his home-office, buried in the work he brought home. His wife has learned to serve him meals there and the kids have learned they're risking their lives if they walk in on him for any reason less than a real emergency.

- When he's home, he picks up the phone on the first

ring—and he can stay on it for hours, doing business, often late into the night.

• Give him a mountain of volunteer work, or better yet two. Pit him against a team of people. Give others a lighter load. No matter. No amount of work is too much for him. Ask him to empty the oceans or count the sand grains in the Sahara. He can do it, even if—and especially if—others can't.

How to spot him (or her) at work

• He works longer than anyone else, and produces more. He needs very little sleep, very little food, and not much human contact. He's absolutely relentless.

• When he finishes one project, he can't wait to take on another one—larger and more difficult if possible.

• He's like a mailman: neither rain, nor sleet, nor snow, nor for that matter a large and vicious dog, can stop him from completing his tasks. He is inexhaustible.

• He works faster than anyone else. "Need those thousand letters filed in an hour?" "Need that fifty-page report finished by lunch?" "Need two years worth of research finished in a week?" Just watch him go. Watch his mind race, watch his fingers fly, watch his wheels turn. No one can do it faster, no one. He is a blur.

• He never hesitates to make impossible demands of others, intruding into their off-hours or private lives without hesitation. His subordinates often feel overwhelmed and inadequate, and cut off from a fulfilling personal life.

• He's contemptuous of nine-to-fivers.

• He can handle more responsibility than anyone else.

Give him twenty-five people to manage. Pile on responsibility for the annual report. Stick him with marketing a new product. Tell him to collect the fees at the parking garage. Simultaneously. He can do it, or at least he thinks he can.

4. The Lone Ranger

> *There is no human problem that could not be solved if people would simply do as I advise.*
>
> —Gore Vidal

How to spot him (or her) at home

• He's emotionally distant. He seems to enjoy being by himself more than with others.

• Family gatherings and social events aren't his cup of tea. He absolutely hates parties, even birthday parties.

• He makes all the major decisions himself and plenty of the minor ones. He's likely to resent attempts to help him.

How to spot him (or her) at work

• He doesn't delegate. He doesn't give younger people a chance to prove themselves or to grow, because he's doing everything himself. He brushes advice aside.

• He announces decisions, rather than seeking other opinions. He doesn't have many—if any—real friendships among colleagues or subordinates.

• He is a famously poor listener.

• He believes in himself. He is not mired in self-doubt, not that anyone can tell, anyhow. So he is very persuasive. It's hard for people who are unsure of themselves to stand up to him.

5. The Puppet Master

How to spot him (or her) at home

• He tries to control everything—from the color of the new car, to the dinner menu, to his daughter's hairstyle, to his son's college choice, to his wife's volunteer activities.

• He owns the remote control, the cell phone, and the thermostat.

• The family computer is used according to his rules. The dog is walked according to his schedule.

• When everything isn't just right—meaning exactly the way he wants it—he goes ballistic.

How to spot him (or her) at work

• He believes the only right way to do things is his way. He does not tolerate errors or delays.

• He criticizes often and unmercifully. And he remembers forever who's screwed up.

• He knows who's late or absent—and lets them know he knows.

• His staff fears his judgments. Subordinates often feel like punching bags. They celebrate Friday and dread Monday.

• Office griping is at epidemic levels. Good people leave frequently.

6. The Hall-of-Famer

> *Between flattery and admiration there often flows a river of contempt.*
> —Minna Antrim

How to spot him (or her) at home

- He acts like royalty, demanding that his needs be met: his slippers brought to him, the newspaper delivered to him unopened, his favorite dishes cooked for him, his clothes promptly cleaned.

- His needs supersede the needs of his spouse or his children. It's his appointments that can't be changed, his word that is final.

- It's his house, his money—and his rules that must be obeyed.

How to spot him (or her) at work

- He's the person for whom the saying, "rank has its privileges" was written. The first privilege is respect from everyone who speaks to him, whether or not he deserves it. The second is the best, which is what he gets: the best seat on the plane, the biggest limo, the most luxurious hotel room, the best service at the restaurant—service that discreetly acknowledges his special status and refined tastes.

- He is unembarrassed when people defer or kowtow to him—he feels he deserves nothing less.

- He takes credit for any of his group's accomplishments, however small his contribution.

• He believes he's exempt from many social conventions, such as telling the truth, keeping his temper, waiting his turn, treating others with consideration.

• He soaks up flattery like a desert cactus, believing everything he hears, even from a regiment of favor-seekers, each trying to outdo the other.

• He always feels he deserves more—more money, more fame, more honors, more titles. He expects to leave his mark on the world.

The superman-complex personality

OK, we've dissected the superman complex according to its six pillars. Now let's look at it in another way, as a personality type of its own. In my experience, people who have the superman complex also have what I call a superman-complex personality.

If you don't know a person well enough to be sure he or she has the six pillars of the superman complex—or if it's yourself you're unsure of—look for the following personality traits. If you find more than a few, you have good reason to suspect a superman complex.

• They're demanding

I know of many a CEO who doesn't hesitate to call his assistants—and expect them to drop everything—24/7/365, even on national holidays. Scrooge, you'll remember, was furious that Bob Cratchet was taking time off for Christmas.

• They're rude

Superman-complex types speak their minds. They say exactly what they think. Normal manners just don't apply to them, since they are "special cases." I know of one executive, for instance, who, when he gets bored with a phone conversation or needs to move on, simply interrupts with a "good-bye" and hangs up.

- **They're condescending**

People with superman complexes genuinely believe they are better than the rest of humanity in all important respects. Realizing that it would be cruel—or seem arrogant—to let others know how they feel, they do their best to conceal their belief in their superiority. But people who work or live with superman-complex types are invariably the target of their concealed contempt, especially when the stakes are high, or in the heat of battle.

> *I have unlearned contempt. It is a sin that is engendered earliest in the soul, and doth beset it like a poison worm.*
> —N. P. Willis

- **They're fault-finding**

Superman-complex types are the proofreaders of life—their life, your life, everyone's life. They can spot your errors and mistakes at greater distance than the Hubble Telescope. And they're more than willing to tell you about them, privately or better yet, in a crowd—all in the name of honesty. All too often, by the way, this same urge toward honesty does not apply when it comes to compliments or recognition of a job well done.

- **They're impersonal**

It's hard to genuinely be friends with people who have the superman complex, because they rarely let anyone get that close. They keep their guard up because they are unwilling to admit their doubts and fears, even to themselves—the very qualities that would make them warm and human. What they do permit is occasional moments of great camaraderie during times of triumph or tragedy. But this openness closes as quickly as a paper cut.

- **They're abrupt**

Superman-complex types aren't generally chatty. They don't have time for gossip, speculation about the weather, or a review of the local team's latest victory. They have more pressing matters to deal with, or they act like they do even when they don't. So subordinates quickly learn that if they have a great story to tell and they're looking for an audience, the person with the superman complex is not a good candidate. He'll interrupt, he'll show his impatience, he may even walk away—unless he's intensely interested in what he's hearing because it could have an important impact on his work or his life.

- **They're moody**

Sometimes they're happy, even momentarily carefree; other times they're depressed or anxious. You never know, because even they frequently don't know where their moods come from. Sometimes their moods are triggered by some event, good or bad. But people with a superman complex can easily be in bad moods when they should be delighted and delighted when they should be terrified. This unpredictability can make them impossible to deal with.

- **They're dogmatic**

The Pope, as we all know, can issue infallible rulings and opinions. Unfortunately, he isn't the only one. Anyone with a superman complex has the same power, or assumes he does. I know one executive, for instance, who, after making a very dubious statement, often says—and quite sincerely, "That's not just my opinion, that's the truth." Oh yeah? People with superman complexes don't offer opinions, they issue edicts. You'd be a fool to challenge them, partly because disagreeing shows how little you know, and partly because if you keep it up, you'll have your head handed to you.

> *Dogmatism is puppyism come to its full growth.*
> —Douglas Jerrold

- **They're certain of themselves**

Very often, you can spot someone with a superman complex because they act without hesitation or doubt. Ordinary mortals may have to stick a toe in the water, but not them. They just jump in, sure they are right, knowing they are invulnerable, convinced no harm will come to them. When it does, it's never their fault.

- **They don't like to give credit**

People with a superman complex turn failing companies around. They bring hit products to market. They're the president of six different clubs. They get masters' degrees while parenting three children and holding down a responsible job at the same time. Maybe they have lieutenants. Or protégés. But they like taking credit for their accomplishments. It's one of the superman complex's main rewards. They're generally not eager to share.

- **They're easily angered**

If you work or live with someone who has a superman complex, you've probably seen him lose his temper all too often. You've probably been the butt of his anger. It is fearsome—thunder and lightning dispensed from on high. It can be triggered by, well, not much at all. A moment's frustration. An underling's error. A bit of bad news. People with a superman complex not only anger easily, they feel free to express it fully, because they don't have to obey normal social rules, not being ordinary mortals.

> *There's man all over for you, blaming on his boots the fault of his feet.*
> —Samuel Beckett

- **They're domineering**

Superman complex types take charge . . . of the boardroom, the jury room, the dining table, the bedroom, the vacation, the shopping trip. You name it, they're boss. They don't take orders. They give orders. That's because they're suited to command. They have what it takes. If you're in the room at the same time, you look to them for direction.

- **They're hard to please**

People who have a superman complex know what they want: they want it their way. They want the report triple-spaced in twelve-point type, not double-spaced in eleven-point (that would be wrong). They want the kids in bed and asleep by 8:30, not 8:31. They want pinpoint cotton shirts, not broadcloth, or 200-thread-count cotton sheets, not a polyester mix. They want the telephone on the right and the notepad on the left. They have opinions and tastes and preferences about practically everything and they want it their way. No other will do.

- **They rarely apologize**

People with the superman complex usually don't admit they're wrong. Not even to themselves. They don't apologize for a combination of reasons. To apologize, they'd have to treat the other person as an equal. To apologize, they'd have to actually feel sorry. To apologize, they'd have to show weakness—at least, that's what many people with superman complexes feel.

- **They're unforgiving**

Elephants' memories are feeble compared to the memories of people with superman complexes—especially when those people are somehow wronged. They don't forget it when you make a mistake. They don't forget it when you forget something you shouldn't. They don't forget it if they think they detect even a whiff of disloyalty. They don't forget it if you vote against them, speak against them, argue with them, or otherwise try to thwart them.

- **They're impatient**

The time of people with superman complexes is more valuable than yours. That's why they don't have much time for you. They don't have much time for anyone, even themselves. They're in a hurry. They have accomplishments to achieve and problems to solve and every minute wasted is a tragedy. So they can forgive themselves for being impatient: it's a minor vice they trade for a major virtue. At least that's the way they see it.

- **They're selfish**

I know one executive—head of a small company—who closed down a branch office but refused to give the office manager severance pay because he went home at five o'clock and didn't work weekends. That was his rationale, but it wasn't his real reason. His real reason—never stated—was that he didn't want to give her any more money. He wanted it for himself. After all, he was the superman in the organization and he deserved as many rewards as he could get. Are you thinking of asking your superman-complex boss for a raise? Watch out. If it's coming out of his pocket, he'll find a dozen reasons to deny you—usually by reminding you of your multiple flaws, mistakes, and failings. When you leave his office, you'll be glad you're not fired.

To reiterate: what I've painted here is the superman complex at its most intense. Not everyone with a superman complex has all of these signs and symptoms. And even those who have them don't act this way or treat people this way all the time. Their superman-complex behavior may be balanced by genuine—and sometimes remarkable—accomplishments, or other positive traits.

But if this description generally fits someone you live with or work with, you can be pretty sure you're dealing with someone who has a superman complex.

Quiz: Do you have the superman complex?

1. No one at my company works harder—or better—than I do. (t) (f)

2. My opinions and decisions are correct at least 90 percent of the time. (t) (f)

3. There are two ways to do any job, a) perfect and b) useless. (t) (f)

4. I can do with less sleep, less food, less leisure than almost anyone else. (t) (f)

5. Faced with a decision, I always make it quickly and confidently. (t) (f)

6. When I set my mind to something, nothing can stop me. (t) (f)

7. Truth is, I could do everyone else's job if I wanted to. (t) (f)

8. My salary, my title, and my awards demonstrate my worth. (t) (f)

9. I've never met a challenge I didn't relish. (t) (f)

10. It's lonely at the top, but I'm comfortable with that. (t) (f)

Scoring the quiz: Do you have the superman complex?

Give yourself one point for every true answer.

9–10: You're the reason I wrote this book, my friend.

7–8: Face it: you have a healthy superman complex.

5–6: You have a superman complex, but you're fighting it.

3–4: You have some superman complex symptoms, but they don't control you.

0–2: You're not suffering from a superman complex—in fact, you may be underestimating yourself.

Quiz: Does your boss have the superman complex?

1. He (or she) is still working when you leave and already there when you arrive. (t) (f)

2. He is the final authority on all matters. (t) (f)

3. He is minimally interested in other's opinions, advice, or help. (t) (f)

4. He tends to take credit for everything good that happens. (t) (f)

5. He tends to blame everyone, except himself, for mistakes or failures. (t) (f)

6. He controls everything in the office, from buying staples to designing products. (t) (f)

7. He intimidates even his peers. (t) (f)

8. He makes impossible demands of his subordinates. (t) (f)

9. He insists on always being treated like a VIP. (t) (f)

10. He accepts nothing less than perfection. (t) (f)

Scoring the quiz: Does your boss have the superman complex?

Give one point for every true answer.

9–10: Your boss is a classic case. Sneak a copy of *The Superman Complex* into his briefcase, the top drawer of his desk, under his copy of the *Wall Street Journal*, and into the seat pocket in front of him on the company jet.

7–8: Your boss has several of the six pillars of the superman complex. He is a bona fide danger to his mental and physical health and yours. Get help.

5–6: Your boss has a partially formed superman complex. Help him change some of his bad habits.

3–4: Yes, your boss has a superman complex trait or two, but he's probably bearable.

0–2: Hardly any signs or symptoms of the superman complex here. Consider yourself exceptionally fortunate.

Chapter Five:
Where Does the Superman Complex Come From?

> *Nothing is so difficult as not deceiving oneself.*
> —Ludwig Wittgenstein

When I decided to write about the superman complex for *Inc.* magazine, the editors sent a young writer to interview me. He started by telling me that, of course, he wasn't an entrepreneur and therefore didn't have a superman complex and couldn't really relate to what it was all about.

"Don't be too sure," I said. "After all, the reason your magazine is interested in this story is that the superman complex isn't just about me."

"Well," he insisted, "it doesn't apply to me. I've never been through any of the stuff you've been through."

"Is that right?" I said. "Well, I read your bio before you arrived here. You've got some pretty impressive credentials of your own. I noticed you'd gotten your undergraduate degree from Harvard. That's a tremendous accomplishment."

"Thank you," he said.

"Let me ask you something. How old were you when you decided that you wanted to go to Harvard? Were you just running around out playing ball one day and said, 'Gee, I think I'll go to Harvard'?"

He kind of shrugged.

"Come on, now," I prodded. "How did it happen? Was it your own decision? Was it somebody else's idea that you go to Harvard?"

"To be honest with you, it was my dad's idea."

I nodded. "So your father wanted you to go to Harvard. Do you mind if I ask how old you were when your dad made this decision?"

"Pretty young actually. Like grade school."

"Okay, now," I said, "tell me how you felt when you first realized that's what you had to do in order to measure up in your father's eyes—go to Harvard. What was it like when you realized how smart you had to be, how well you had to perform?"

As I gazed into his eyes, he got that look on his face that everybody gets when his soul is being exposed. When the real core truth is surfacing.

"It was terrible," he said. "It was an unbelievable burden."

"And you carried it with you every day and every night, right? Every test wondering whether it was good enough, every semester, every time report cards came out. Every year, every new teacher assignment, every class ranking that came out, every PSAT and SAT test, you revisited the same fear—what if I'm not good enough? What if I don't make it? What if I don't live up to my father's expectations?"

And now the tears started coming down his cheek. And so I said in the most compassionate way that I could, "Don't tell me you don't know about the superman complex."

"I see what you mean," he said quietly.

I've told you this story because it illustrates one way we get our superman complexes—by trying to live up to the expectations of others. I've seen this not only in my own life, but in the lives of many other people who have the superman complex.

But it is only one of many factors in our makeup and our experience that contribute to this collection of unfortunate habit patterns I call the superman complex.

In my experience, it's rare to find the superman complex in people without genuine ability. When you see it in people who have hardly any skills or smarts, it's because they've completely lost touch with reality.

So the superman complex is strongest in people whose claim to superman status isn't all that unreasonable: smart, capable, energetic, often charismatic people. They look at their many good qualities and inflate them. They whiteout their flaws and weaknesses. They become convinced that they *are* what they so much want to be: superhuman.

Why? Why do some people contract a permanent case of superman complex while other, apparently quite similar people escape it entirely or get cases as mild as the common cold?

I believe the superman complex has a two-part origin. If people have only one of the parts, they'll probably escape the worst of it. But if both sources are at work, the chances of escape are just about nil. The complex cannot be avoided. It must be cured, or at least forced into remission.

What are the two parts?

Part one: human nature

Although we may argue about the details, everyone knows there's such a thing as human nature: a certain basic set of behaviors that we all share, more or less. One of the most obvious, for instance: mother love. Practically every mother feels it; there's no way to turn it off. And for those rare individuals who don't have the feeling, there's no way to install it after the fact.

Human nature, apparently, is built-in, hardwired. But where does it live?

It's in the genes

Evidence is growing that human nature is in our genes—at least in part. Every few months, it seems, scientists claim to find a gene for one trait or another: shyness, violence, alcoholism, just to name a few.

While the geneticists are peering at our chromosomes through their microscopes, searching for evidence of inherited traits, the social scientists are looking at the whole person sitting across from them and finding—guess what?—the same thing. For instance, they've discovered startling similarities among identical twins who were separated from birth. My favorite example involves two middle-aged English women who were adopted by two different couples when they were only a few weeks old and raised in opposite ends of the country.

When these two ladies finally met each other a couple of years ago, they arrived at their meeting place wearing practically identical brown tweed suits. In their first conversation, they discovered some striking similarities. Both hated the water—bathing beaches, that is. Yet both went frequently, to be with friends. Both dealt with their fears by *backing* into the water, until it was up to their knees. Each could stay in the water only for about five minutes.

Now if either one—but only one—of these women had gone to a psychologist, he might have looked for a childhood trauma to explain these actions. He probably would have concluded neurosis was the cause. He might have designed a course of behavior modification to eventually eliminate the behavior. But the fact that both twins shared the identical symptoms and they'd been raised in different homes without even knowing the other existed makes the cause almost certainly, if surprisingly, genetic.

If this were the only such coincidence, maybe you could dismiss it as just that—coincidence. But a huge, long-term study of separated twins at the University of Minnesota uncovered all kinds of startling and, if genetics were ignored, inexplicable coincidences. Among them, the same breed dogs as pets, given the same names; wives with the same names; children with the same names and ages; identical jobs; identical tastes in clothing; identical religious and political viewpoints; identical nervous ticks—and some of these from twins raised on different continents!

In fact, the scientists running this study found that *every single personality trait* they could identify had a better than fifty-fifty chance of being shared by both twins. The only possible explanation: it's in the genes.

Will scientists someday find genes that control the degree of ambition we have? Our ability to focus? Our capacity for leadership? Our stubbornness? Our charisma? Our quickness to criticize? Our willingness to work? Maybe so.

But the scientists who study twins have discovered something almost as important as the notion that personality and character have genetic origins. They've discovered that while our genes might *predispose* us to certain characteristics, they definitely do not *predetermine* what we will become. Those identical twins separated at birth do *not* have identical personalities or characters, even when they share many similar traits. One might have a trait totally absent in the other. A trait may be very strong in one twin, but far weaker in another. The combination of similarities and dissimilarities results in people who are reassuringly individual.

It's in the subconscious

> *The subconscious is ceaselessly murmuring, and it is by listening to these murmurs that one hears the truth.*
> —Gaston Bachelard

A totally different set of scientists . . . and psychologists . . . and philosophers looks at the origins of personality and character in an entirely different way: as a product of the brain's subconscious makeup. This leads to a totally different view of where the superman complex might come from.

For example, Sigmund Freud believed that the unconscious was a vast reservoir of instinctual drives and a storehouse for all the thoughts, wishes, and urges we want to conceal from our conscious awareness because they cause conflict—the little boy reaching into the cookie jar, momentarily frozen by the conflict between his conscience and his sweet tooth, for instance, or a man with a superman complex dealing with his fears of slothfulness by working harder than anyone else.

Freud thought the human psyche was composed of three interlocking, interacting parts: the *id*, the instinctive part, a kind of selfish, demanding child who wants and wants and wants, no matter what's possible; the *ego*, kind of a servant to the id—trying to meet its demands, at least as much as the real world allows; and the *superego*, the conscience, which tries to keep a lid on the other two by imposing the moral standards that come from society at large.

Freud says that when the ego can't meet the demands of the id, we feel anxious. When the ego goes overboard, we feel guilty or ashamed. The ego creates defense mechanisms to deal with these feelings, including 1) repression (the bad stuff goes under the rug), 2) regression (we act like children), 3) reaction-formation (we deny the truth), 4) projection (we blame someone else), and 5) sublimation (we put a good twist on bad feelings—hitting a tennis ball, not our bosses, for example).

In Freud's terms then, the superman complex is a kind of multifaceted defense mechanism that includes repression, regression, reaction-formation, projection, and sublimation.

An executive with the superman complex might deny he always changes his mind, for instance (repression), or he'll have full-blown temper tantrums over minor issues (regression), or deny the validity of bad news (reaction-formation), or he'll see his own faults in someone else (projection), or get obsessed with jogging (sublimation).

To my mind, Freud's model makes good sense. It helps us understand ourselves better. But it is not gospel. It is basically a very insightful way of looking at the way human beings act, nothing more or less.

> *A certain degree of neurosis is of inestimable value as a drive, especially to a psychologist.*
>
> —Sigmund Freud

Successors to Freud

The psychologists who came after Freud modified his ideas in ways that would have astounded, dismayed, and infuriated the most famous shrink of all. For the most part they tended to downplay the demands of the id and credit the ego with the ability to create, plan, and form reachable goals entirely on its own. Also, they've come to credit social relationships with a major role in personality development.

One famous psychologist, Alfred Adler, proposed a theory that may have a lot to do with the superman complex. He noted that all children are born with a deep sense of inferiority because of their small size, physical weakness, and lack of knowledge. This feeling motivates them to strive to achieve competency, meet the challenges in life, and try to be better than other people. It's easy to see how this impulse—exaggerated by circumstances—could lead to a superman complex. In fact, when I read about Adler's theory, I was reminded of my own days on the football field at Columbia.

Another psychologist, Karen Horney, theorized that personality was the product of childhood social experiences, especially with parents. She held that when parents are indifferent, disparaging, or inconsistent, the child feels helpless and insecure—with a basic anxiety and a basic hostility (toward the parents). As he grows up, the child—she believed—adopts one of three ways of acting: moving *toward* others, moving *against* others, or moving *away* from others. The person who moves *against* others is attempting to find security through domination. Sound familiar?

The behaviorists

In the early years of the twentieth century, a Russian scientist named Ivan Pavlov trained dogs to salivate when they heard a bell. His work in the field of stimulus-response eventually inspired two American psychologists, John B. Watson and B. F. Skinner, to develop yet another theory of human personality: behavorism. They believed that human behavior was not so much the result of what happened in our subconscious, but what happened to us externally—specifically, what kind of behavior rewarded us and what kind punished us. Over time, we learned to avoid the latter and repeat the former, like rats who avoided the mazes where they got electric shocks and kept going back to those where they found food.

Skinner "proved" his theory by using rewards and punishments to treat smoking, overeating, nail-biting, classroom disciplinary problems, alcoholism, even littering in public parks. His methods often worked—and still do.

And some superman-complex traits could be explained in behavioral terms. For instance, the *know-it-all* may have gotten that way by being praised by parents and teachers for knowing the answers. In the same way, the *glutton for punishment* may have been rewarded for hard work. I can easily imagine the *Lone Ranger* being praised when he accomplished something "all by himself." The *hall-of-famer* may have adopted that behavior mode when he found the only way he could get approval from his parents was by bringing home prizes and awards, or getting his name on the honor roll.

Behaviorism may account, in part, for elements of the superman complex. But it's obviously not the whole story. Today few psychologists believe that behaviorism totally explains how people act. They usually mix in healthy helpings of social influence and the operations of the subconscious.

> *If we ever do end up acting just like rats or Pavlov's dogs, it will be largely because behaviorism has conditioned us to do so.*
>
> —Richard Dean Rosen

Trait theories

Okay, one more possible way of thinking about human personality: trait theories. Roughly, it works this way: people are kind of like dog breeds. They come with certain personalities. Poodles are smart, yippy, and demanding; St. Bernards are plodding but loyal; pit bulls are vicious.

According to the trait theorists, human beings can be divided into personality breeds in much the same way, although the traits aren't necessarily passed down directly from parents to children. And, of course, human personalities are a lot more complicated than dog personalities.

The idea of categorizing people by personality type dates back several millenia, to the pre-Christian Middle East. There so many ways to do it that I'd need another book to list them all. And all of these theories are a lot better at describing people than explaining why they act the way they do.

The oldest of the trait theories is the so-called "Enneagram"—from the Greek word for *nine*. This system of classifying people may have originated with the Magi. Certainly it was expanded and modified by the philosophers, theologians, astrologers, and scientists of ancient times, including Pythagoras, the Sufis (the mystics of the Moslem faith), and the Kaballah, a Jewish mystical work.

In recent times, the Enneagram was brought to the attention of Western psychologists, theologians, and philosophers by George Gurdjieff (1869–1949), an Armenian priest and mystic. In his hands, it was not only a system for classification, but also a way to understand behaviorial motivations and treat character and personality imbalances. The modern Enneagram holds that nine distinctive patterns of unconscious motivation explain why we do what we do. They are: 1) achiever, 2) helper, 3) succeeder, 4) individualist, 5) observer, 6) guardian, 7) dreamer, 8) confronter, and 9) preservationist. How we combine these various tendencies determines what we are.

One of these patterns—the achiever—comes very close to what I call a superman complex. According to the Enneagram theory, achievers are perfectionists, workaholics, critics, high-energy born leaders. When they have these qualities in moderation, they can live in balance. When these qualities are exaggerated or distorted, they're constantly on the edge of disaster.

Part two: the environment

> *If we ask for help, it is a sign of weakness, dependency on another man or woman: we've failed.*
> —Frank Pittman

It's in the upbringing

Most of the highly successful, high-achieving people I've met or have read about come from families that have preached the virtues of achievement for generations—passing on these values in much the same way religious faith gets passed on. You could say they're only doing what their parents told them to.

Lee Iacocca, the former chairman and CEO of Chrysler, for instance, devotes much of the first chapter of his autobiography to a description of his family life, and describes, in particular, the "ambition" and "hope" that motivated his father, Nicola, who had first come to America in 1902, at the age of twelve.

And Noel Tichy, in his book about Jack Welch Jr. and General Electric—*Control Your Destiny or Someone Else Will*—attributes much of Welch's success to Welch's mother, Grace, whose parents had been Irish immigrants and who herself never graduated high school. According to Tichy, Welch often talks about his late mother with "unabashed emotion." "She felt that I could do anything," Welch has said in describing his childhood. "If I was having trouble in algebra or something, she'd say, 'Just go upstairs and study. You can do better than anyone.'"

Both my parents were from immigrant backgrounds—my father's family was from Ireland, my mother was a first-generation immigrant from Germany—and both of them, like Iacocca's father and Jack Welch's mother—were ardent and passionate believers in the American Dream. They had the first car in our neighborhood in Queens, New York—a 1950 Hudson.

Whatever we did—whether it was the subjects we studied in school, the sports we played, or the chores we did at home—my brothers, my sister, and I were always urged to try a little harder, to do a little better. It was our parents' way of telling us that there was no ceiling on our potential. We could be whatever we wanted to be, whatever we were willing to work hard to be.

Ours was a traditionally structured family: each of us had our "jobs." My father's job was to be the breadwinner. My mother managed the household. And our job, as kids, was to always do our best, whether our parents were at home or at work.

If you're inclined toward a superman complex (if it's in your genes), what your parents teach you, what they expect from you, and what they need for you can either help you keep these inclinations in check or strengthen them. In my case—and I think this is probably true for most people whose superman complexes come to dominate their lives—my upbringing strongly encouraged my tendency to see myself as more capable, more focused, and more motivated than most people.

My father and mother told me over and over again that they expected me to always do my very best. The implication was clear: If I did my best, I'd come out ahead of everyone else. I'd get straight A's, I'd win the race, I'd get elected, I'd succeed at whatever I set my hand to. Of course, this was encouragement, but it was much more than that. It set a level of expectation. My parents not only wanted me to do my best, they expected that I would. And they expected that as a result, I would outthink, outfight, outrun, and even outplay anyone I competed with.

Did this make me fear failure? Of course it did. The last thing I wanted was to disappoint my parents. And so their expectations of me became my expectations of myself.

I could have chosen either of two paths, I suppose. I could have simply decided that all of this was beyond me, that I could never live up to all the expectations and that I could never handle the responsibility. I took the other path: I decided I was more than up to the challenge. I decided that I could do anything. Was I compensating for feelings of insecurity or inferiority? Perhaps. I couldn't afford to have any feelings like that. If I let myself question my abilities, I'd be damaging the self-confidence that drove me and made me capable of doing what I did.

The French philosopher Dennis Diderot once wrote that when they are young, all men—meaning women too—create statues in their minds, statues that bear a striking resemblance to themselves, but are greater and without flaws. Then, they spend their lives trying to live up to this statue.

I think that's what we all do; only in modern terms, we'd say self-image, not statue. We take a, well, generous view of our intelligence, our morality, our ability, our motivation, our relative worth in comparison to the rest of humanity, our judgment, and all of our other qualities. And we have no problem shrugging away our flaws, whatever they may be: selfishness, nasty temper, contempt for others—well, everyone has his or her own list.

We have good—or at least understandable—reasons to see ourselves as better than we are. It feels good, plain and simple. It gives us self-confidence. It helps us establish relationships with people we admire. It gives us a boost in our dealings with the world, whatever they may be. If we're naturally inclined toward a superman complex, we choose to see ourselves as supercapable, supersmart, superquick on the uptake, superalert, superstrong emotionally, and just generally one giant step up the ladder from ordinary folk.

In the back of our minds, somewhere, we know that this self-image—to put it nicely—is something of an exaggeration. We know that the self-image and the person aren't a perfect match. But the self-image is too comforting, too seductive, too reassuring to give up. So we do everything we can to convince ourselves and everyone else that our self-image is a picture-perfect portrait of ourselves.

> *Between ourselves and our real natures we interpose that wax figure of idealizations and selections which we call our character.*
>
> —Walter Lippmann

It's the result of social pressures

Even if we were inclined to back away from this too-perfect version of ourselves, we'd have a hard time doing it. In our highly competitive society, the pressure to be a superman is fierce. Our society insists on separating people into two categories, winners and losers. The winners get the praise and the loot, the losers get the boot, plus the hearty contempt of their betters.

That's how I felt when I didn't make the Columbia traveling squad for the Princeton game. And I imagine that's how every high school, college, or pro football player feels when he's cut from the squad. Not only does he lose the chance for glory, he is humiliated and dispirited.

Among winners, which is how everyone wants to be seen and wants to think of himself or herself, the biggest winner of all is the superman, the person at the very crest of the mountain, who produces more, knows more, works harder, fears less, and does everything better than anyone else, just for a start. Is it any wonder, in our dog-eat-dog society, that this is how we'd like to be seen?

I've made all of this sound pretty nasty, but there's a side to it that's actually quite noble, or at least emphasizes a better aspect of human nature: the search for heroes. Rightly or wrongly, we yearn for heroes. Nations think they need them. Families think they need them. Businesses think they need them. In fact, there's really no aspect of life in which a hero or two wouldn't be awfully nice to have: war, sports, health care, politics, philanthropy, law enforcement, education, religion—the list is endless.

And, needing heroes, we find them. Stop in sometime at your local trophy supply store and you'll see what I mean. Check out a military medals catalog. Watch the Olympics or the World Series or the Super Bowl. Tour a Civil War battleground. Watch the Academy Awards.

When people stand out—in practically any field—we find a way to recognize them. We make heroes out of them. We make them larger than life—Michael Jordan, Steven Spielberg, John Glenn, Colin Powell. We tell ourselves that they are greater than the rest of us and less flawed as well. They are, well, superhuman. And we do the same thing on a local level. That's what all those trophies are for.

People like me, who have a superman complex, see ourselves as heroes as well. A friend of mine calls this "being a legend in your own mind." We want our families, friends, and work associates to think of us the same way. We are heroes because we bought the car for a lower price than anyone else or because we always know the right restaurant, or because we always get the jump on the competition. We're heroes because we always throw completed passes.

And society is delighted to give us the label. Our friends, family, and coworkers want us to be heroes. They want to feel their leader is superhuman. It allows them to feel safe and secure. It gives them coattails to hang onto, an umbrella to stand under. It relieves them of the need to be heroes themselves, which is no small service.

What happens when society finds a real hero, or a reasonable approximation? They're canonized. Books are written about them. They're featured in TV biographies. Their stories are acted out on stage, or made into movies, or taught in school. They become part of history. I'm talking about Hannibal, Jesse Owens, Mozart, Churchill, Mother Theresa, Achilles, Albert Einstein, Florence Nightingale, Babe Ruth, Gandhi, Helen Keller, Douglas MacArthur, Ernest Hemingway, and others of their sort. These are the people we aspire to be: conquerors, philosophers, inventors, geniuses, statesmen. Is it any surprise we squint mightily in the hope of seeing their qualities in ourselves?

Not only do we want to be like them, we should want to be like them, for each one of them in his or her own way, has advanced the cause of civilization. Each has left his or her mark. And it is by the deeds of heroes like these that civilization advances. At least to some extent, their existence puts pressure on us to match their achievements, to equal their wisdom, to measure up to their standard. It provides a ruler we can measure ourselves against, a comparison we cannot escape.

Where does the superman complex come from? It comes from our genes. It comes from our subconscious. It comes from our upbringing. It comes from social pressures. It comes from a combination of influences that none of us can escape.

These influences lead us into a pattern of behavior; they instill in us a set of habits that become so deeply ingrained that we and those around us come to believe that's who we really are. Fortunately, it isn't—as you will see.

We adopt these habits because they offer a big payoff. They provide us with a steady stream of rewards. But they also harm us at home, among our friends, and especially at work. . . .

Heroes are created by popular demand, sometimes out of the scantiest materials.
—Gerald W. Johnson

Chapter Six:
The Ups and Downs of Being a Superman

> *In the United States there's a Puritan ethic and a mythology of success. He who is successful is good. In Latin countries, in Catholic countries, a successful person is a sinner.*
>
> —Umberto Eco

The year was 1975. My career as a navy fighter pilot was over. I needed a job now. So I went to a "job fair" at a big Atlanta hotel, accompanied by several other navy buddies, also looking for jobs. We arrived in our first store-bought business suits, résumés in hand.

One company caught my interest: AON, formerly known as Ryan Insurance Group, one of the fastest-growing insurance consulting firms in the United States. I liked their recruiter's style and swagger. Like me, he was an ex-fighter pilot, Vietnam vet. He'd told everyone his company environment was tough and supercompetitive, almost like he was discouraging applicants. He sounded like a marine recruiter.

I was convinced Ryan was my kind of company. Now I had to convince them I was their kind of guy. My buddy Rick and I stood outside the booth and watched for a while. The Ryan reps were having a great old time giving job-seekers thirty seconds to make their case, then rejecting them. They would have probably rejected me, too, if I hadn't been quick on my feet.

My friend went into the booth first. "Why should we hire you?" the Ryan guys asked.

Rick had a terrific answer. He told the recruiters that he'd had the highest grades in high school, that he'd won all the intramural navy pilot competitions, and, all modesty aside, had to admit he was the greatest navy pilot to come down the pike—combat experienced included.

The Ryan guys liked what they heard. They didn't hesitate to set up an interview. They were so impressed with him, in fact, that they didn't seem the least interested in me. When I stepped up and handed them my résumé, they each gave it a quick once-over and told me distractedly that they weren't interested.

"What do you mean, not interested?" I said, my superman complex stirring.

"Well, we just got the best pilot in the Navy," one of the recruiters said. "Why would we be interested in you?"

"Because I taught him everything he knows." Which happened to be true.

They both laughed and put me on the interview list.

That weekend, the Ryan people interviewed me not once, but several times, and several times more in the next two weeks. Then came the offer. They weren't paying much—less than I could have gotten if I'd gone into commercial aviation—but I was pumped. I accepted immediately.

When I got to Chicago for my two-week sales training program, my manager took me aside. "Carey," he said, "I expect you to finish first in your class. If you don't—well, let me be frank. You'll be through here."

He was trying to push my buttons, and he was succeeding better than he could have imagined. The horrifying prospect of packing my bag and going back to Pensacola, jobless, motivated me to work every bit as hard as I had when fighting for a spot on the Columbia football team or trying to earn my navy pilot's wings. Of course I finished first in my class. My superman complex wouldn't have settled for any less.

I worked for Pat Ryan Associates for six years, steadily climbing the ladder, meeting challenge after challenge and having a great time doing it. I started out as a field rep, sitting in the back office at car dealerships, selling financing, life insurance, disability insurance, extra warranties—sometimes even alarm systems, undercoating, and rustproofing. This job is not for the faint of heart, believe me. There's no merit to it—it's mostly commissions or bonuses, assuming you produce. And some parts of the job weren't strictly on the up-and-up.

The most, well, dubious part: rustproofing and undercoating. At one dealership, a tough old sales vet briefed me on the product they wanted me to push: Ziebart, a combination undercoating and rustproofing. "Chicago has really tough winters," he told me, "so it's the perfect product for us. You ought to be able to sell it to everyone who buys a car from us."

"What does it cost and what does the customer get, exactly?"

"It's $179. For that, if we have time, we undercoat the car with a creosote sealant, spray it from one end to another, into the wheel wells, drill into the door jams and spray inside all the rocker panels. We add a full fifty pounds to the weight of the car."

"Sounds good," I said. "I can sell that kind of value for $179. But I notice you said, 'If we have time.' What if you don't have time?"

The sales manager snorted. "Then we just drill the holes," he said, with a broad wink.

So much for ethics.

I spent the next six months traveling from one dealership to another throughout the Midwest, spending two to three weeks at each, putting in ten hours a day or more. I was determined to become a district manager, and the only way to do that was to bring home the numbers. Every day—and I do mean *every*—Ryan's district manager checked how many products I'd sold and how much profit I'd generated. These daily checkups made me so tense that more often than not, the first thing I'd do every morning was go into the bathroom and vomit.

Still, I loved it! Every morning when I drove up to a dealership, I felt an adrenaline rush that was like flying a combat mission. I loved knowing immediately whether I'd succeeded or failed. I also loved being one-on-one with the customer. I loved trying to figure out what I'd done right when I made the sale—and what I'd done wrong when I didn't. Evaluate. Experiment. Succeed. Fail. Try again. And focus like a laser beam.

Within six months, I was a district manager. My first assignment: the Orlando, Florida, area, which hadn't been meeting its numbers. "Fix it," I was told. "Get those numbers up." Nope, no pressure there, no more than flying over the North Vietnam gunnery school. I went out and hired some guys like me—ex-navy or air force fighter pilots, former professional athletes. They were the players, but I was the coach. If the team kept losing, I knew I'd be the one who'd be cut.

More pressure. An even greater challenge. Not only did I have to motivate myself, I had to motivate others, which was something I'd never been taught. It was sink or swim—and I swam. I set up sales meetings that supercharged everyone. I went into the dealerships and charged up the existing staff. Nothing could stop me, my superman complex saw to that. And Ryan rewarded me accordingly.

After that, more challenges, more rewards, more recognition. Succeeding at Ryan had become the all-consuming life passion—never mind that I had a wife and two daughters. I was a star, a model for new employees, and eventually, a recruiter whose job was to sign on more people like myself.

Ryan had me working seventy- or eighty-hour weeks and loving it—not because he was paying me so much. He wasn't. He was mixing the money with recognition, which is exactly what my superman complex wanted. He was motivating me to get to the top, where all the sacrifices would pay off big-time.

At Ryan and Associates, I'd gotten myself into the position every ambitious person dreams of, through my intensity, immersion, and single-minded focus. I was a gold-plated success and being groomed for even better things. What had happened on the football field, and then in the navy, had happened again. I'd driven myself to overcome every challenge and come out at the head of the pack.

When all goes well for people like me, who have a superman complex, life can be very good indeed—by the usual standards anyhow.

The upside: the external payoff

> *The moment of victory is much too short to live for that and nothing else.*
> —Martina Navratilova

A successful person with a superman complex benefits externally in many ways:

- **Achievement and accomplishment**

In some ways, a person with a superman complex spends his entire life writing his epitaph—or, to be a little less ghoulish about it, his résumé, or the paragraph beneath his picture in the yearbook of life. Accomplishment is what he is all about and awards constitute his middle name.

Superman-complex types build a list of achievements with as much energy and determination as they build a retirement nest egg. Every item on the list is like a piece of expensive clothing. It makes the wearer look good and feel good. It impresses onlookers. It builds an image like nothing else.

- **Power and position**

This is the fundamental reward for people with a superman complex. They get to call the tune. The buck stops at their desk. And that seems only right—if you are a superman, you should have superpowers. You should run your company or department or household. You should oversee those who lack your extraordinary qualities.

- **The respect and admiration of strangers**

Successful people with a superman complex are also rewarded by others' respect and admiration. They get the best table at the restaurant. They sit courtside during the playoffs. They ride in limousines and, if they're high enough on the food chain, private airplanes. Community organizations and nonprofits beg them to be on their boards. They are all but saluted as they walk down the street. How does this feel? Well, it's the next best thing to being a movie star.

- **The satisfactions associated with success and victory**

Think of Michael Jordan's great leap of triumph when he sank the last shot of his career and led the Chicago Bulls, once again, to the world championship. Successful people with superman complexes get to feel that way again and again and again. Essentially, all their efforts, all of their abilities and all of their successes are rewarded by continuous jolts of feeling just plain wonderful.

- **Financial security**

Here's another reward successful superman-complex types get that ordinary people rarely achieve. And it's a big one. Financial security provides freedom. It allows the person who has it to stop worrying about his children or his spouse, to focus his abilities on higher goals, to enjoy his life—if his superman complex will let him.

- **Self-confidence**

Self-confidence is probably the most fragile of human assets. As George Bernard Shaw once wrote, "It is easy—terribly easy—to shake a man's faith in himself. To take advantage of that to break a man's spirit is devil's work." Successful people with a superman complex have their self-confidence bolstered constantly. Each new achievement reinforces their belief in themselves—at least superficially.

- **A good excuse to avoid mundane matters**

Does the king have to take out the trash? Is it right to trouble the queen with filing papers? And even if it is, who'd dare to do it? Rank has its privileges, as they say in the military, and what rank is higher than superman (or woman)? People with the superman complex, even when they're not particularly successful, demand and usually receive a trunk full of perks: no menial chores to worry about, no errands to do, assistants eager to take care of their personal needs.

The internal payoff

In addition to the tangible payoff, every superman-complex type who succeeds is also on the receiving end of some big-time *intangible* benefits.

The most important of these: successful people with superman complexes are free to let these feelings and attitudes dominate their lives. They're free to work as hard as they want, to try to control everything in view, to do without sleep, to make snap decisions about everything, to bear the heavy burden of being right all the time.

People in this situation have no pressing reason, and probably no time, to examine their lives, to rethink the way they act or the way they treat people. They can just keep on doing what they've been doing, beyond criticism—or at least effective criticism. Their success protects them—and isolates them—from others. In short, for someone with a superman complex, success can be permission. That's a great benefit, when you consider all the perks involved.

The downside of being a superman

> *The world is divided into two categories: failures and unknowns.*
> —Francis Picabia

But what about failure? Failure sometimes happens to people with superman complexes. However they may feel about themselves, they are only human and therefore imperfect. And in the event of failure, the critical weaknesses in the superman character become readily apparent.

Poor delegator

Because people with superman complexes are so convinced of their capabilities, they are often terrible delegators. This is a big problem in business, to say the least. "When you want something done right, do it yourself," say people with a superman complex. And they go even further. When they want something done at all, they do it themselves.

It goes without saying that this mode of behavior wastes the talents of colleagues or family members. It can also stretch to the breaking point the ability of someone with a superman complex to achieve his goals. Enough of this straw will break any camel's back.

A corporate CEO with this weakness can seriously damage his company, even though his conscious motive is to help it in every possible way. Besides squandering the talents of others, by trying to do everything himself, or to take responsibility for everything, micromanaging, he encourages good people to change jobs, to look for personal fulfillment elsewhere.

Poor team player

People with a superman complex have another weakness, related to but somewhat different from their problems with delegating. They are frequently very reluctant to ask for help. That increases their load—and their chances of failure.

From the corporate standpoint, this kind of CEO is a bad bargain. He's a soloist, in a part that calls for an orchestra leader. No matter how capable he is, he's a disaster waiting to happen, both for his company and for himself personally. He is a prime candidate for overload and meltdown.

Crisis mentality

Another inherent weakness: as I've said, people with superman complexes are often so certain they're on the right course that setbacks take them by surprise. And a surprise is very disconcerting to someone with a superman complex. It trashes his plans. It mocks his intelligence. It may cause him to panic. Unpleasant surprises make the superman type feel as though he's losing control, or intolerably out of balance. That could trigger either frantic—and borderline irrational—activity . . . or paralysis.

Executives with superman complexes sometimes have breakdowns in these situations. They sometimes walk out without warning. They fire everyone in sight. They come home and take out their tensions on their family. They drink.

President Richard Nixon's staff developed a strategy to deal with their boss when unpleasant surprises inspired him to let loose a barrage of irrational orders ("Have his taxes audited! Tap his phone! Leak dirt about him to a reporter!"). They agreed to do what he wanted. Then they held off for a few days, until Nixon regained his equilibrium. Once that happened, he was grateful he hadn't been obeyed—if he remembered giving the command at all.

A series of unexpected setbacks may well leave someone with a superman complex essentially disabled, unable to collect himself, unable to bounce back. Not good for the company or family he or she is managing.

People with superman complexes know they have these weaknesses, although probably not consciously. This knowledge causes anxiety, apprehension, uneasiness—a generalized feeling, even when everything is fine, that trouble is just over the horizon.

This is one of the downsides of having a superman complex. It's one reason people who suffer from the condition work harder and longer and try so desperately to control everything and everyone. They're trying to protect themselves from failure.

Upside/downside—does it really matter?

When they succeed, then, people with a superman complex rake in the rewards. When they fail, they take it hard. But does that really matter? I don't think so. In the largest sense, I believe, people whose lives are run by their superman complexes lose out on much of the best life has to offer, even when they are very successful.

> *We are all failures—at least, all the best of us are.*
> —J. M. Barrie

Chapter Seven:

What's Wrong with Being a Superman?

I've flown combat in Vietnam and I've started my own business. You want to know which is more frightening? Starting your own business. It isn't even close. I'm not sure why this is—maybe it's because if you buy the farm in combat, you're gone. But if you buy the farm in business, you're still there. You just wish you weren't.

Whatever the explanation, if you have the superman complex, entrepreneurial terror threatens you at a deeper level than combat terror. In combat, all you're risking is your life. When you're starting your business, you're risking your identity, your self-image, your belief in yourself, your reputation, the respect of others. You may also, depending on how you financed it, be risking your house and, possibly, your marriage.

When I founded my business—and quickly got into financial trouble—I found that coming home without a paycheck was a lot worse than trying to avoid my first surface-to-air missile in a combat mission over Hanoi. After all, it hadn't been my fault that the guy on the ground was shooting at me. He was just doing his job. But it *was* my fault when I didn't bring any money home to my family.

For someone like me, who has the superman complex, the fear of failure—the fear of not being a good father or a successful breadwinner—is especially intense. When you go into business, it's a feeling you live with 24/7.

Yes, combat involves gut-wrenching terror. But it only lasts a short time. They shoot a missile at me, I see it, I turn hard to avoid it, I watch it explode harmlessly, I'm okay, I can breathe. Then I fly back to the ship, have a hot meal, sleep in a warm bed, have twelve hours aboard in complete peace.

But entrepreneurial terror—the fear of failure, of letting your family down—is constant. It's with me every day, every night, at home, at work, at play. It's like a giant tidal wave, forever threatening to engulf me.

An exaggerated fear of failure is one price we pay for having the superman complex. There are many others. . . .

The dark side of being superman

> *Perpetual devotion to what a man calls his business is only to be sustained by perpetual neglect of many other things.*
> —Robert Louis Stevenson

Sounds like a good idea, being a superman. There's nothing we can't do, nothing we can't accomplish. Everyone respects us, in fact, obeys us. We are recognized and rewarded. We're important people. What's wrong with that? Well, nothing—if that's all there was to being superman.

Problem is, being superman has a downside that makes the good parts look like the tip of an iceberg. Just below the waterline, there are enough drawbacks to sink a fleet of Titanics. And if we're not careful, these drawbacks could sink us as well.

Of course, depending upon the magnitude of your

superman complex, you're not likely to suffer all of these problems all of the time. But I'm willing to bet you're afflicted with more of these drawbacks than you want, probably more than you're willing to admit.

Self-inflicted wounds

Chances are, if you're suffering from a superman complex like mine, you will sooner or later—and probably sooner—end up doing yourself some serious damage. Not just in one way, but in several.

• You put your mental health at risk

It's not easy being a superman type. We tend to worry a lot. We worry that something might go wrong or that we might fail. We worry that other people might let us down. We worry that we've missed something crucial. We even worry when we're sleeping.

Chiefly, we worry about tomorrow. In fact, we think about tomorrow so much that we're hardly aware of today. We worry about bills coming due, or that we'll be faced with something even we can't handle. We worry that everything will come apart.

We also worry that we'll be unmasked—that people will at last discover that we're not the superman we're pretending to be, not as smart, not as able, not as *right* about everything. We worry that someone will see through the façade and reveal the real us.

To avoid this at all costs, we impose rigid discipline on ourselves. We work as much as humanly possible and maybe a bit more, and we chew ourselves out without mercy if we catch ourselves relaxing. We feel guilty when we're not doing our job—working, juggling the kids, advancing on the enemy, patrolling the beat, rewriting the proposal, finding the bleeder and tying it off.

As for having fun—well, fun is for other people. We can go through the motions when we have to, but we seldom simply enjoy ourselves wholeheartedly. Fun isn't productive. Fun doesn't get us any closer to our goals. It doesn't pay the bills. Besides, if we let ourselves have fun, something dangerous might sneak up on us.

This is one of my worst problems. I have a very hard time relaxing and having fun, and I'll bet you do too. I try to combine fun and business—socializing with a client, for instance, or negotiating a contract over lunch at a good restaurant. I might even look like I'm having fun, but I'm not fooling myself. I'm working. Enjoying the meal is so secondary I hardly remember it afterwards. I'm so busy saving the world I don't have time to savor it.

> *All animals, except man, know that the principal business of life is to enjoy it.*
> —Samuel Butler

Quiz: Can you let your hair down?

1. I tell a joke at least once a week. (t) (f)

2. I wish there were more casual dress days at work. (t) (f)

3. I really enjoy playing with the dog. (t) (f)

4. I have been known to sing in public (church doesn't count). (t) (f)

5. When my ten-year-old says "damn," I'm more likely to laugh than scold. (t) (f)

6. I sometimes hold hands with my spouse in public. (t) (f)

7. The last time it snowed, I threw a snowball at someone. (t) (f)

8. In warm weather, I like riding in a convertible. (t) (f)

9. I can't resist good chocolate. (t) (f)

10. I'd have a good time playing co-ed volleyball on the beach. (t) (f)

Scoring the quiz: Can you let your hair down?

Okay, now give yourself one point for every (t) answer.

9–10: You're refreshingly uninhibited and happy to be yourself.

7–8: No one would mistake you for a party-pooper.

5–6: You probably come across as a little stiff.

3–4: Take off that tie (or those heels) and join the party.

0–2: You are a forbidding presence.

Despite all of our hard work, the light at the end of the tunnel never seems to get any closer. Our goals are always beyond our reach. The image that comes to my mind is being trapped in a hamster cage on an exercise wheel, unable to look anywhere but straight ahead, running as fast as possible and not moving forward an inch.

After I hit the wall and stopped running long enough to honestly inventory my emotions—which is not something superman types like us are likely to do, except when the end of the world seems near—I didn't like what I found.

The first emotion I came across was feeling out of balance, like I might have taken off the training wheels a little too early. It was as though I was frantically making corrections, but I wasn't sure I was doing the right thing at the right time and I knew I might fall over any minute.

I discovered that most of the time, I was *afraid.* Mainly afraid of failing, but also afraid I would be unmasked, or that the sky actually might fall and I would be helpless to save myself and everyone else.

I also discovered that I was *angry.* At what? Well, it seems to me (and to everyone else) that I was mainly angry at people. Screw up or disappoint me in some other way and my anger was out of the holster, blasting holes in you. No one was immune—family, friends, employees, the waitress, the cab driver, the woman behind the airline counter, and any car that dared to pass me.

When I thought more about my anger, I realized something was wrong. How could I be angry at *everyone?* Did no one measure up to my standards? That wasn't logical. I asked myself who I really was angry at. And you know what? I came up with someone: me.

Why was I angry at myself? The best answer I've been able to come up with is that I was angry because I didn't like the life I'd locked myself into. I didn't like getting up in the morning and going to work. I didn't like thinking my life would be this way until I retired, assuming I made it that far.

Of course, I wasn't always angry. Sometimes, my feelings were reversed, by which I don't mean happy. I mean depressed, because in emotional coinage, depression is the obverse of anger. Anger is a way of sharing your misery. Depression is what happens when you turn it all on yourself.

> *What I've learned about being angry with people is that it generally hurts you more than it hurts them.*
>
> —Oprah Winfrey

Quiz: How much peace of mind do you have?

1. I usually sleep well. (t) (f)

2. I often "replay" past conversations in my mind over and over again. (t) (f)

3. I'm always worried—sometimes more, sometimes less. (t) (f)

4. Part of my body is always in motion (scratching, tapping, leg jumping, etc.). (t) (f)

5. Sometimes I get the feeling people are being "careful" with me. (t) (f)

6. When I drive, I never let anyone get the better of me. (t) (f)

7. Most people don't get to the point fast enough. (t) (f)

8. How my food tastes is very important to me. (t) (f)

9. I frequently listen to and enjoy music. (t) (f)

10. I usually shrug off little irritations. (t) (f)

Scoring the quiz: How much peace of mind do you have?

Give yourself one point if you answered (t) to questions 1, 8, 9, and 10 and one point if you answered (f) to questions 2, 3, 4, 5, 6, and 7.

9–10. You have the peace of mind of an Indian mystic.

7–8. You're better off than most, but there's room for improvement.

5–6. You're about average and that's no reason to celebrate.

3–4. You're probably just hanging on, feeling life is rotten.

0–2. You are a volcano filling with lava. An explosion is imminent. Nearby populated areas should be evacuated.

- **You damage your psychic health**

> *Nothing is so difficult as not deceiving oneself*
> —Ludwig Wittgenstein

What do I mean "psychic health"? I'm talking about something more profound than mental health. I'm talking about sense of self or self-worth. I'm talking about the deepest part of us, our core—not about transitory emotions.

I believe that those of us who let our superman complexes run our lives are risking our psychic health, our very sense of self, because we are engaged in a massive act of self-deception. We're fooling ourselves.

How so? The six pillars of the superman complex help us create a flawless—but fictitious—self-image. It is this self-image we present to the world and to ourselves. But it's distorted because it omits our flaws, weaknesses, and vulnerabilities. It denies our needs and our feelings. It leaves out our softer side, the human side.

Remember Professor Marvel, the old carny fraud played by Frank Morgan in the movie version of *The Wizard of Oz*? In the early scenes, he was the seedy but kindly old humbug who advised Dorothy to go back home to Auntie Em. Later, in the Emerald City, he was the man behind the curtain, the con artist who tried to convince Dorothy, the Tin Man, the Cowardly Lion, and the Scarecrow that he was "the great and powerful Wizard of Oz."

Well, that's us. We're the fellow behind the curtain, busily moving the levers, flashing the lights, booming our voices through the loudspeaker, and generally trying to look like more than we are.

Where's the problem here, if we can keep it up, if no one looks behind the curtain? Well, there are several:

• Creating this self-image and foisting it on the world is an admission that we fear the real us isn't good enough. Professor Marvel is barely a shadow of the Great and Powerful Wizard of Oz.

• Even if the self-image we've constructed fools everyone else, it doesn't fool us. We know, somewhere within, that it's bogus. We tell everyone to "Ignore that man behind the curtain" but we can't ignore him. Others may think we're the Wizard, but we know better.

• We're exhausting ourselves frantically moving those levers back and forth, turning the lights on and off, and booming our voices out of the loudspeaker. This reduces our efficiency, productivity, and energy.

• We're trying to do things that might be within the Wizard's power, but are beyond ours. Truth is, we don't know how to send Dorothy home. Like Professor Marvel, we don't know how to work the hot-air balloon. But we can't admit it to anyone, so we have to try to do it anyhow.

• If we're loved, or respected, or even feared, it's not for who we are, it's for who we pretend to be. So we never feel genuinely loved, respected, or feared.

• Because we're projecting this fierce, false image, we can't let anyone—including ourselves—see some of our best and most genuine qualities—for instance gentleness, caring, willingness to compromise.

• Because of the image we're projecting, we can't let anyone—ourselves included—know when we need help, or comfort, or encouragement.

• If we pretend long enough, we may have trouble remembering that there's a man behind the curtain, the real us. The more we pretend to be the autocratic father, the overburdened CEO who has to be treated with kid gloves, the guy who's always right, the VIP who always comes first, the less we are in touch with our true feelings, motives, goals, and needs.

This last one is a biggie. After decades of pretending to be the Wizard, both to ourselves and others, we have a hard time knowing who we really are. We have trouble being anything but inauthentic, people with phony laughs, phony concern, phony politeness, phony values, an empty feeling inside, and a vague sense of discomfort living within our own skins.

When the superman complex is in control, and we're behind the curtain, busy trying to look like the Wizard, we are not operating according to our internal values. We're not generating any respect for ourselves because we know we're not who we appear to be. That makes us terribly dependent on others' esteem, approval, and admiration. Others' opinions of us—which are usually based on our material achievements—become a substitute for self-esteem and self-respect. That perpetuates the superman complex within us and makes us less human than we would be otherwise.

> *Let the world know you as you are, not as you think you should be, because sooner or later, if you are posing, you will forget the pose, and then where are you?*
>
> —Fanny Brice

- **You damage your spiritual health**

When we are totally in the grip of our superman complex, we don't have much room in our lives for any higher power. I'm not just talking about bosses, police officers, city or town officials, the IRS, our lawyers, our doctors, our bankers—although most of us have trouble with people in this category.

The higher power I'm talking about is God.

A belief in God requires at least a little humility. We superman-complex types rarely manage to display much of that. We can do anything, remember? We can move mountains, at least figuratively. We can accomplish more than ordinary mortals, or so we tell ourselves and anyone else who needs to hear it. We have the last word about all things concerning ourselves because we think we're the ones who are all-powerful.

But what if, in our heart of hearts, we believe? What if our inner self is in conflict with the self we present to the world (and try to sell to ourselves)? In that case, we have trouble. We have a spiritual disconnect—uncertainty, confusion, doubt. We cannot ask for help, because we're busy insisting help is the last thing we need.

When it comes to our spiritual health, then, letting our superman complex run our lives is a bad bargain at best. We're trading what may be life's greatest gift for hollow pretense.

Quiz: Who reigns supreme in your universe?

1. I pray frequently—and sincerely. (t) (f)

2. I often consult advisors about emotional matters. (t) (f)

3. If people would just follow my advice, their lives would be better. (t) (f)

4. There are several people in my life I trust completely. (t) (f)

5. I often teach, but seldom learn. (t) (f)

6. I can easily fall asleep in an airplane. (t) (f)

7. Sometimes, I just let things happen. (t) (f)

8. When people point out my mistakes, I often laugh—and always admit them. (t) (f)

9. I am the smartest person I know. (t) (f)

10. I consider myself extremely self-sufficient. (t) (f)

Scoring the quiz: Who reigns supreme in your universe?

Now, let's score it.

Give yourself one point if you answered (t) to questions 1, 2, 4, 6, 7, and 8. And give yourself one point if you answered (f) to questions 3, 5, 9, and 10.

9–10: You are humble and human.

7–8: You know you have betters, although you probably couldn't name them.

5–6: Maybe you're not king of the mountain, but you're at least prince.

3–4: You know you're the leader of the pack and so does everyone else.

0–2: You worship at the church of you.

> *Belief consists in accepting the affirmations of the soul; unbelief, in denying them.*
> —Ralph Waldo Emerson

- **You damage your relationships with others**

When we let our superman complexes rule, we not only distance ourselves from any religious beliefs we might have, we distance ourselves from those around us, at work, at home, in social situations, even at play—to the extent that we allow ourselves to play.

The reasons are several:

- We don't let people know us. That's partly

because we don't know ourselves, being unable to see past our own pretense, and, to the extent we can, not wanting others to see what we think of as the weak, flawed, uncertain real person behind the curtain.

• We have no real confidants. We rarely, if ever, let our best friends, our spouses, our parents know what really drives us, or why we are acting the way we are. We really don't want confidants, because we feel that our secrets are too shameful to share, sometimes even with ourselves.

• We do not trust people. They constantly disappoint us. They fail. They forget. They are incompetent in our judgment. So we conclude trusting them would be foolish, even dangerous. If we actually trusted someone, we might be inclined to tell them our secrets, which is out of the question.

• We live within a shell that's hard to penetrate, cutting ourselves off from certain emotions—sentiment, silliness, nostalgia, love, joy, contentment, peacefulness. Whatever soft side we have, we keep to ourselves. The result: people may respect us, they may even admire us, but they seldom love us.

• We let ourselves be easily offended. We don't like people laughing at us, or criticizing us, or telling us the truth if it differs from our truth. And so people aren't genuine with us. They watch their tongues. They're guarded. They practice their remarks in advance.

• We rarely savor our relationships. We're too busy, too focused on the task at hand, too consumed with moving ahead and doing what we feel needs to be done. And the people in our lives know this.

They know we're not willing (or not interested enough) to give them our full attention for very long. We are available only in snatches.

> *It is an equal failing to trust everybody, and to trust nobody.*
> —English Proverb

Quiz: Do people really know you?

Ask a friend or coworker (not your spouse—that would be too easy) to take this quiz and answer these questions about you:

1. He (or she) generally votes a) Republican, b) Democrat, c) Independent, or d) "for the best person."

2. He is a) not at all, b) mildly, or c) very religious.

3. If he could buy only one CD, he would choose a) Bach, b) the Beatles, or c) Gershwin.

4. He exercises a) not at all, b) occasionally and reluctantly, c) regularly, or d) obsessively.

5. He is generally a) optimistic, b) pessimistic, or c) realistic.

6. He prefers a) action/adventure, b) comedies, c) psychological dramas, or d) quirky independent films.

7. Give him two weeks off and a ticket to anywhere and he'll go a) to a great beach, b) to explore an exotic country, c) trekking, d) on a cruise, or e) to a sophisticated foreign city.

8. What basketball, baseball, and football teams does he follow and root for?

9. Is he happy with his job?

10. What aspect of himself would he change if he could? a) weight, b) age, c) education, d) marital status, or e) wealth

How to score the quiz: Do people really know you?

Give yourself one point for every answer your friend or coworker gets right.

9–10: You are a very open person.

7–8: You're not all that guarded, but you could be a little more forthcoming.

5–6: You don't go out of your way to reveal yourself.

3–4: You are a mystery to most people. Is that really necessary?

0–2: Compared to you, the Sphinx is a blabbermouth. Why all the secrets?

• You risk your physical health

If our superman complex is strong enough and relentless enough, we are compelled to forge on, to the detriment of mind and soul—and, ultimately, body.

If there's one single characteristic that practically everyone with a superman complex has in common, it's that we work long hours (for pay or not, doesn't matter.) We rise early, we work endlessly, we stay late, we work on weekends, we take few vacations, or we take working vacations. No surprise here. We think we're supermen. Other people may get tired or hungry, other people may need a break, other people have to rest occasionally, or sleep in—not us. We're above weaknesses of that sort.

Trouble is, we may believe we're supermen, but our bodies know better. They know, even if we don't, that we're human—nothing more, nothing less. They know we have our limitations and our weaknesses. They know we get tired, and hungry, and that sooner or later, we will crash.

People like us, who carry the superman complex monkey on our backs, endanger our health in several ways:

• We work all the time except when we're sleeping and we keep that to a minimum. No, not everyone with a superman complex does this—just 90 to 95 percent of us. We ignore our bodies' urgent requests for simple leisure, lying around, doing nothing, or playing.

• We are always in a hurry. Don't you wish the day had forty hours and the week had ten days—at least? Well, let's hope that doesn't happen, because if by some miracle it did, we'd just work even longer.

• We are driven to use every moment productively. Trouble is, we don't recognize that productivity comes in several flavors. Some productivity contributes to work, and some to just plain living.

• We can never completely relax. What's the purpose of relaxation anyhow? It's just a waste of time, right? Wrong. Something pretty wonderful happens when we relax. We're reborn a little. We recuperate from the day's strains and bruises. In fact, relaxing restores our strength so that we can be—you guessed it—more productive.

Where does all this lead us? It makes us sick. It gives us stomach problems, back problems, high blood pressure, and who knows what else. It gives us insomnia. It causes eating problems. If we're standing at the edge, it pushes us over, into a nervous breakdown or burnout.

Whatever our superman complex may be doing to our minds, it is torturing our bodies. When we let it rule our lives, we're shortening our lives and risking our lives at the same time.

Ironically, the net effect of all this hard work is that our ability to work hard is damaged and diminished. It's a fitting punishment, I guess, but why are we doing this to ourselves?

> *The feeling of being hurried is not usually the result of living a full life and having no time. It is on the contrary born of a vague fear that we are wasting our life.*
>
> —Eric Hoffer

Quiz: How well do you take care of yourself?

1. I do not smoke cigarettes or cigars. (t) (f)

2. My weight is right for my height and age—or better. (t) (f)

3. I exercise at least twice a week. (t) (f)

4. I frequently eat chicken, turkey, and fish. (t) (f)

5. I sleep at least seven hours a night, on average. (t) (f)

6. My partner and I are pleased with our sex life. (t) (f)

7. I have plenty of energy to play with my kids. (t) (f)

8. I have a thorough medical checkup yearly. (t) (f)

9. I almost never get too drunk to drive legally. (t) (f)

10. My blood pressure is fine. (t) (f)

How to score the quiz: How well do you take care of yourself?

Give yourself one point for every true answer.

9–10: You're the envy of all of us wrecks.

7–8: Not bad, but you could be better.

6–7: Join the club; wait, you're already in it.

4–6: Face it: you need repairs.

0–3: You're showing symptoms of the superman complex—you're very likely a glutton for punishment, a Lone Ranger, or both. And you're paying a serious physical price.

If we let our superman complexes run rampant, we face the prospect of slow-motion self-destruction. It's a high price to pay, I think, even for a pile of achievements, a big bank account, and the respect of your peers—especially if you can have all that without committing a kind of psychic suicide. I'll get to that later.

Unfortunately, the high price we pay personally for our superman complex isn't its final cost. To tote that up, you have to include the damage our superman complex does to others. That damage is enormous and pervasive, in both major arenas of life, the workplace and our home lives.

• The damage we do at the workplace

In the workplace, the person with a superman complex is like a bull in a china shop. Every step is accompanied by the sound of crashing dishes. But in the workplace, that crashing sound is coming from the hopes, the self-esteem, and the morale of coworkers and employees. This loss takes several forms. Not every one of them fits everyone with a superman complex, but I'll bet you recognize yourself in some:

• When we let our superman complexes run rampant, we hog the decision-making power, stealing it from employees and coworkers who have enough stature and ability to make their own decisions. It's our way of maintaining control, which may satisfy our needs, but doesn't contribute to the growth of the people we're controlling.

• We stifle the talents and contributions of our employees and coworkers. When our superman complexes are in full display, we scare people off. They don't want to risk getting their ideas stuffed down their throats. Their survival instincts protect them. Their fear cheats them out of opportunities and it cheats us out of their help and creativity.

• As a corollary, we cheat our organization, wasting its human resources—human resources, I might add, that the company probably found only after great effort and pays highly for. This is another consequence of the inability of that superman within us to trust anyone.

• We tend to kill the messenger. You know the wise-ass remark, "My mind's made up, don't confuse me with the facts"? Well, when our superman complexes are in high gear, we do a variation: "I know the truth—contradict me at your own risk." We know, or so we think, that our plan is the right plan, that we've thought out every detail, that success is inevitable. So we're likely to shoot first and ask questions later of anyone who brings back the news that something has gone wrong.

• We discourage genuine successors. It happens all the time in corporate America: the ambitious second-in-command leaves in frustration because the aging CEO won't retire. Our superman complexes somehow convince us not only that we are indispensable, but that our reigns need never end. But, as the old saying has it, "Cemeteries are filled with indispensable people." The result: when it's time for even superman to call it a day, no one's there to take over.

• We damage the self-esteem of our colleagues and employees. First, we criticize their performance: No matter how hard they try, they never quite manage to live up to our standards. They make mistakes, they fail, they overlook something, they're not fast enough—and we relish chewing them out. Sometimes we even lie in wait, then pounce. We are the judge and jury, they are the ones who stand accused. Second, we criticize their characters. We make them painfully aware of their flaws, shortcomings, and weaknesses. We let their strengths go unmentioned.

• We make employees and coworkers dependent on us. We spread a minefield—tasks, opportunities, initiatives—in front of them, then tell them they have no chance of making it through safely unless we take them by the hand and lead them through it, one baby-step at a time. We make sure that whenever they confront minefields they come a-running, panic in their eyes. We treat them, in other words, like children, errant children, never allowing them to grow up.

• We make the work lives of those around us miserable. We criticize, we shout, we accuse, we throw temper tantrums, we change our minds for no good reason, we belittle, we strut, sometimes we are so obnoxious that if we weren't the boss, someone might punch us in the mouth. We generally act as though we are better than other people, which of course we think we are.

• We ask the impossible. We think nothing of requiring our employees to work evenings or weekends. We call them whenever the urge strikes us. We toss them the scut work, bales of it. We ignore whatever life they might have in their off hours, except for infrequent and obligatory comments like, "How's that wife of yours?"

This kind of behavior has consequences. It magnifies workplace anger and resentment, it leads to absenteeism and increases turnover. It triggers sabotage, both the conscious variety and the unconscious variety. In the end, it undermines what you're trying to do.

If we had no faults of our own, we should not take so much pleasure in noticing those in others.

—La Rochefoucauld

Quiz: Do you have a superman complex at work?

1. Some of my work colleagues are social friends as well. (t) (f)

2. I dispense praise and criticism about equally. (t) (f)

3. I know the names of the wives and all children of the people I work with most closely. (t) (f)

4. My subordinates never conceal bad news from me. (t) (f)

5. Business is important, but coworkers' personal lives come first. (t) (f)

6. People I work with tend to ask me to lunch. (t) (f)

7. I am careful about making too many demands on my people. (t) (f)

8. Turnover and absenteeism aren't a problem at my office. (t) (f)

9. When people come to me with ideas, I make it a point to hear them out. (t) (f)

10. I often ask coworkers for help. (t) (f)

Scoring the quiz: Do you have a superman complex at work?

Give yourself one point for every true answer.

9–10: You are a saint.

7–8: You're a warm and decent human being.

5–6: Your coworkers see you as a mixed bag—bearable but annoying.

3–4: Many are angry with you and resent you.

0–2: Whenever you're out of earshot, people are bitterly griping about you, at work . . . and probably at home as well.

- **The damage we do at home**

Can a leopard change its spots? Can someone with the superman complex be a lion in the workplace but a pussycat at home? I suppose it's possible to totally compartmentalize yourself, but it's mighty difficult. And probably beyond most of us.

The superman complex isn't like a suit jacket that we wear on selected occasions but otherwise leave on a closet hanger. It's less detachable even than our underwear. Most times, we're still wearing it when we crawl into bed. At least that's my experience, and if you're ruled by a superman complex, you can probably say the same.

So those of us who are dominated by our superman complexes are superman at home as well as at work. We are just as knowledgeable, just as capable, just as much in command, just as dedicated to the tasks at hand as we are at work. What's wrong with that? What's wrong is that we hurt the people we care most about in life and damage our relationships with them.

• We encourage dependency. When we're always right and we're always in control, what's more natural than for our spouses and our children to consult us before making any decision, especially an important one? The superman within us may say that's the way it should be, because we always know which choice is right. One question: who's going to make the decisions when we're not around? Who'll have the nerve, the knowledge, and the maturity? The answer is, no one—not if we don't let them learn how.

• We stunt the intellectual and emotional growth of our children. By constantly belittling, correcting, finding fault, and tyrannizing, we plant and fertilize the seeds of self-doubt and low self-esteem. It's not truth that hurts, it's truth delivered thoughtlessly and with cruelty.

• We don't give our family members the opportunity to live their own lives. We live their lives for them, choosing their friends, their boyfriends or girlfriends, deciding how they spend their money (or the money we give them), dictating what they do with their time ("No rock concerts for you, young lady!" Or, "You will not be allowed to quit your piano lessons, young man!" Or, "You're going off to play golf when the garage looks like that?" Or, "If you spent a little less time at the mall, maybe dinner would be on time.") We treat our spouse and children and sometimes our friends as though they were our subsidiaries or servants.

• We put distance between ourselves and our family members. Who wants a hug from someone who yells at you all the time, who always calls you a screw-up or who constantly berates you for being late? How can you have an intimate discussion with someone who is convinced that when the two of you disagree, you're wrong and he or she is right. Always. How can you depend on someone's support when that person constantly finds fault with you?

• We encourage defiance and rebellion. What makes children rebel? What makes spouses spend money they don't have, or go fishing when they should be staying home? At least in part, they behave irresponsibly because it's the only way they can be themselves, the only way they can slip out from under the thumb of someone like us, who—driven by our superman complex—can't resist making rules and trying to enforce them.

• We make family and friends miserable. People talk secretly with each other about how to deal with us. People signal each other, warn each other, that is, about our current mood. We argue, we shout, we demand, we complain, we lash out, we disapprove, we accuse and generally give ourselves permission to act in ways we wouldn't tolerate in anyone else.

When a man spends his time giving his wife criticism and advice instead of compliments, he forgets that it was not his good judgment, but his charming manners, that won her heart.

—Helen Rowland

Quiz: Are you the CEO of your family?

1. I seldom share major decisions with my spouse. (t) (f)

2. Sometimes I must refuse my kids' requests so they know who's boss. (t) (f)

3. My house has a strict set of rules and everyone obeys them. (t) (f)

4. Children have to earn their privileges. (t) (f)

5. I manage and distribute all the money. (t) (f)

6. I tell family members what to wear and how to cut their hair. (t) (f)

7. When I'm in the car, I always drive. (t) (f)

8. If anyone asks my kids who's boss at home, they always say that I am. (t) (f)

9. The rest of the family handles all petty household chores. (t) (f)

10. Extended family gatherings always take place at my house. (t) (f)

Scoring the quiz: Are you the CEO of your family?

Give yourself a point for every question you've answered (f).

9–10: You understand the meaning and the spirit of democracy.

7–8: You slip occasionally, but your heart is in the right place.

5–6: A power struggle is going on in your family. Is that what you want?

3–4: You've got them under your thumb, for better or worse.

0–2: You learned about human relations in business school.

- **You endanger your future**

All of this adds up to something we superman-complex types don't even want to consider, much less believe. At its worst, the damage we do to ourselves—and the damage we do to others because we are fiercely pretending to be more than we actually are—threatens our futures, both in business and in our personal lives.

How so?

First, because we continually operate beyond our abilities. No one—repeat, no one—can do everything. No one can always be in total control. No one. No one is better at everything than anyone else. No one. Sad to say, human beings have many attributes, but omnipotence is not one of them. And yet our superman complex tells us that we're an exception. "No one" refers to everyone else, except us.

That means trouble. Because we overestimate our abilities, or knowledge and even our endurance, because we operate under the conviction that we have no limits. We take on tasks that no one can handle, we put unbelievable pressures on ourselves, we stretch mind and body to the breaking point—and beyond.

And if we keep at it long enough, we fail.

Second, we endanger our futures because we isolate ourselves, emotionally, intellectually, psychologically. We're flying blind and we won't allow ourselves a copilot. Tell me, would you like to approach a carrier at night, in rough seas and high winds, in that condition? I sure wouldn't. And yet I lived my life that way for years. Everyone suffering from the superman complex lives his or her life that way, at least to a degree.

Quiz: Are you setting yourself up for failure?

1. I don't ask for help—I don't need it. (t) (f)

2. I'm always willing to take on one more task. (t) (f)

3. There's nothing I can't do if I put my mind to it. (t) (f)

4. My people can always work harder if necessary. (t) (f)

5. Everybody thinks I'm really pretty amazing. (t) (f)

6. I'd rather die than fail. (t) (f)

7. I always make sure every little thing is taken care of. (t) (f)

8. I do not allow my subordinates to argue with me. (t) (f)

9. I'd rather do it myself than accept mediocre work from a subordinate. (t) (f)

10. I reward subordinates well and expect total loyalty and availability. (t) (f)

Scoring the quiz: Are you setting yourself up for failure?

Give yourself one point for every true answer.

9–10: Now playing in your crystal ball: scenes of imminent self-destruction.

7–8: You're headed for the brink. Pull back now or else.

5–6: You're biting off more than you can chew—unless you're really superhuman.

3–4: You may be managing, but you're asking for trouble.

0–2: You have the right attitude for success.

Chapter Eight:

Is There a Better Way to Live?

Sometimes, insight into your soul comes at the most unexpected times.

Let me take you back to the fall of 1972. Vietnam. My buddies and I were flying combat over heavily defended targets in North Vietnam daily, risking our lives. We'd gotten into a pattern. We'd destroy all the strategic and tactical targets we could find, then North Vietnam would call for negotiations. The U.S., as a gesture of goodwill, would call off most of the bombing.

While the negotiators talked for a week or two, the North Vietnamese rebuilt and resupplied what we had destroyed. When they were back up to strength, they stopped negotiating. And pretty soon, we were called in again, to destroy exactly the same targets we'd taken out a month earlier, putting ourselves at risk again, taking losses again.

After enough of this, it became clear to all of us pilots that our country wasn't really trying to win this war. It had other, far vaguer political objectives in mind. It was a devastating realization for a bunch of young, wide-eyed, bushy-tailed, apple-pie-and-mom patriots. Our nation was using us for cannon fodder. How could we keep going, being brave, being courageous, risking our lives again and again to keep hitting what we believed was our enemy?

We desperately needed something to motivate us, something worth fighting for, something worth facing death for. But what? We talked about it again and again, and pretty soon, more than enough reason to keep fighting just bubbled right up.

Many of our fellow pilots, our friends, our buddies, had been shot down during the course of the war. Most were captured and were languishing in a jail we called the Hanoi Hilton. The more we thought about them, the more we realized we *did* have a reason to fight. Our reason: to force North Vietnam to release them.

And that—rather than winning the war, which seemed to be out of the question—became our mission. We committed ourselves each and every day, each and every night, to fight for our imprisoned comrades in arms. We flew with renewed courage and determination until, finally, that day came. The prisoners were released.

I can't hope to describe how we felt when we got to meet with them, hug them, share a beer with them. It gave meaning to everything we'd done, every risk we'd taken, every life we'd lost. It was like victory.

And we made a startling—and extraordinarily satisfying—discovery when we talked to them. It seems that their captors had told them the United States had stopped fighting, that the war was over, that they'd been abandoned. Then they'd hear *our* bombs dropping, and see the flash of the explosions—and they knew we were still there. And that gave them the will to survive. In a wonderfully serendipitous way, they had given us something to fight for and we had given them something to believe in.

What in the world does this story have to do with the superman complex? It has *everything* to do with it, because it demonstrates more dramatically than anything else I have ever heard a way of finding satisfaction in life that transcends your own personal needs and desires.

For most of us, life is a constant pursuit to satisfy our personal needs and desires—not just our material wants, but our psychological needs. For people with the superman complex, that's what success is all about.

The biggest problem with success is that one success is never enough. In fact, twenty consecutive successes or fifty or whatever number you name are not enough. Those of us who base our identity on our success are playing a very dangerous game. If we fail—even if we battle to a standstill—we risk our self-respect. We no longer know who we are exactly. We need another success and another and another after that to remind us and revive us.

Don't get me wrong. Success is not bad. It is very good. It translates into material comfort and security, not only for yourself, but for those around you. It puts food on the table and cars in the garage. It sends your children to school. It is not to be sneezed at. But it is not to be worshipped either. It is not an absolute necessity.

So what is a necessity? What do human beings need in order to be fully human, in order to completely experience the richness of life and find life satisfying? In my opinion, no one has answered this question better than the late Dr. Abraham Maslow, in his book *Toward a Psychology of Being*.

Abraham Maslow's insights

> *There must be more to life than having everything.*
> —Maurice Sendak

Dr. Maslow proposed that human beings had a "hierarchy of needs," from the simplest to the most complex, and that people couldn't even try to satisfy the more complex needs until the simplest ones were met.

This is his hierarchy, beginning at the bottom rung: physiological needs, like food and rest; safety needs, or basic physical security; love needs, or feelings of belonging and appreciation; esteem needs, both from ourselves and others; and finally—

Self-actualization

The need for self-actualization is the desire to become more and more what we are, to become everything that we're capable of becoming. People who have met all their other needs, who in essence have everything they need, can focus on maximizing their potential. They can seek knowledge, peace, esthetic experiences, self-fulfillment, oneness with God.

When people achieve self-actualization, according to Dr. Maslow, they have "peak experiences." Peak experiences are those transcendent moments—unfortunately they rarely last longer than that—in which we have a profound sense that all is well, that we are truly in tune with the world, that we have a handle on the mystery of life. For most people, these moments, if they occur at all, are not only brief but rare—perhaps three or four times in a decade.

But even when self-actualized people aren't experiencing those rare "peak experiences," they go through life generally accompanied by a sense of well-being, a sense of purpose, a sense of satisfaction with what they're doing.

I do not believe our superman complexes can give us that feeling. They can give us a few moments of triumph. They can temporarily boost our egos. They can allow us to buy things that impress others. But they cannot give us a continuing sense of fulfillment. In fact, they make it impossible for us to feel fulfillment.

What can? Where then should we turn for satisfaction and fulfillment in life? To God, many people would say, and I believe they are right. But I'm asking a somewhat different sort of question: how can we use our God-given talents and abilities to find true fulfillment?

Where can you find fulfillment?

> *Happiness is an imaginary condition, formerly often attributed by the living to the dead, now usually attributed by adults to children, and by children to adults.*
>
> —Thomas Szasz

People have asked this question for, well, as long as there have been people. All kinds of answers are floating around out there, but none have gotten universal approval.

I could leave it at that without feeling ashamed of myself, but I will rush in where angels fear to tread. I have a notion I want to share with you about how to find fulfillment in life. It works for me and for some others I know. It might very well work for you too.

The best thing about it: you don't have to do anything different. You can do exactly what you're doing now. All you have to do is adopt a different attitude, to look at what you're doing from a different perspective. Here's the attitude I suggest: *Think of everything you do in terms of serving others.*

• Delivering a speech? Think of how you can actually *help* or inform the people in your audience.

• Cooking something? Think of how you can *please* those who'll be eating the meal.

• Firing someone? Think of how you can *serve* him, how you can help him.

• Making a sale? Think of what your product or your service can do to *serve* your client.

• Giving directions? Think of what you can do to *help* the other person do what needs to be done quickly, easily and with a minimum of grief.

• Making a deal with another company? Think of yourself as *serving* the people in your company—and the other company as well.

I'm not suggesting that you do anything different. I'm just suggesting that before you do it, you ask yourself, "Who am I serving?" and "How can I serve them best?"

Of course you won't be serving the same people all the time. Sometimes, you'll be serving your family or specific family members. Sometimes you'll be serving your friends. Sometimes you'll be serving your company or your department or your clients or consumers. What matters is that you are NOT serving *yourself.* You're not asking yourself, "What do I get out of this?" You're asking what the people you're serving get out of it.

Stephen R. Covey calls this process "making deposits in the emotional bank account," and says it's the basis of win-win business relationships. You're not figuring out "how I get mine." You're figuring out how they get theirs. You're not manipulating people so you come up with the big end of the stick, or the awards or the bonuses.

I'm saying watch out for the other guy's win, not your own. Don't give away the farm—that's lose-win and that wouldn't serve your family or your employees. But concentrate first on making sure the other person gets his or her fair share or reward.

I know. Heresy, at least in some points of view. This is definitely *not* looking out for number one. Or at the very least, it doesn't look like looking out for number one. It looks impossibly unselfish, unrealistically altruistic. But it is not. That deserves repeating: this is not naive altruism.

I could make a good case for it not being altruism at all.

If you concentrate on serving other people rather than focusing on your own needs, you'll get two different sorts of payoff.

First, I've found you'll get what you deserve, what's fair, or what you've earned. The people you're serving will make sure of that. You'll have your success and everything that comes with it. You may have more than you would otherwise, because people will *want* to do business with you.

Second, you'll have the continual satisfaction of helping other people. You'll have the pleasure of seeing them succeed or thrive because of you. You'll have the gratification that comes from helping them have what they need. This is a greater gratification, please believe me, than simply succeeding on your own.

I know one man who gets up a half hour earlier than he has to every morning and calls five people he knows who are having problems and offers them help. Imagine the feeling he gets back when even one of those people overcomes his problems as a result.

As you know, there's nothing new about what I'm saying. It's one of the basic building blocks of Christianity and plenty of other religions as well. It's also at the heart of a lot of humanist philosophy. So I'm not exactly the first person to discover the benefits of serving others.

I'm putting the idea in a new context. I'm saying that there's a better way to live and do business than by putting your superman complex in charge. Your superman complex, in addition to all the damage it does to you and the people around you, can never give you anything more than a temporary pleasure fix, like a bite of candy.

But if you put your superman complex out to pasture, and concentrate instead on serving others, you'll eventually find that you don't need the fixes. You'll feel a sense of fulfillment and well-being that's on a totally different level. Won't do any harm to your business results either. I say this because it's happened to me—and not just me.

> *At some moment I did answer Yes to Someone—or Something—and from that hour I was certain that existence is meaningful and that, therefore, my life, in self-surrender, had a goal.*
> —Dag Hammarskjöld

Living life as though you'll do better next time

If you're anything like me, you're probably thinking, "This all sounds nice. Maybe there's even something to it. Someday I should give it serious consideration."

Why not now? I believe too many of us are living our lives as though we'll do better next time, which is a pretty risky strategy at best.

Those of us who suffer from a superman complex are not likely to be meeting all the needs on Maslow's scale. That last rung on the scale—self-actualization—is currently out of our reach. We're barely able to get a few fingers on the rung below it. If that isn't a good reason to take aim at our superman complex today and not a minute later, I don't know what is.

Quiz: Are you enjoying life?

1. I wake up looking forward to the day. (t) (f)

2. I get great satisfaction and joy from my family. (t) (f)

3. These are the most productive years of my life—so far. (t) (f)

4. If I met someone just like me, I'd enjoy spending time with him. (t) (f)

5. I'm almost never bored, even when I'm doing nothing. (t) (f)

6. I've found a good balance between work and personal life. (t) (f)

7. There's plenty of love in my life, in both directions. (t) (f)

8. My responsibilities are well within my ability to handle them. (t) (f)

9. I'm interested in all kinds of different things. (t) (f)

10. Sometimes I'm nostalgic, but the future interests me more than the past. (t) (f)

Scoring the quiz: Are you enjoying life?

Give yourself one point for every true answer.

9–10: You are definitely smelling the roses.

7–8: Life probably feels pretty darn good to you.

5–6: Here's where most people are, swimming in a mixture of good and bad.

3–4: Life is a grind, but not without its rewards.

0–2: You deserve better. Everyone deserves better.

Redefining success

You know the business cliché: "The definition of crazy is when you keep doing the same things but expect different results."

As long as we let our superman complex call the tune, we're reluctant even to consider changing. We'd rather redouble our efforts, we'd rather keep doing what we've always done, only faster and better, because we're still counting on success to provide us with true fulfillment.

I say the superman-complex definition of success is the wrong definition of success, even though it happens to be the standard "dictionary" definition. I think I've found a much better one:

"He has achieved success who has lived well, laughed often and loved much; who has enjoyed the trust of pure women, the respect of intelligent men and the love of little children; who has filled his niche and accomplished his task; who has left the world better than he found it, whether by an improved poppy, a perfect poem, or a rescued soul; who has never lacked appreciation of Earth's beauty or failed to express it; who has always looked for the best in others and given them the best he had; whose life was an inspiration; whose memory a benediction."

—Betty Anderson Stanley. reprinted by the syndicated advice columnist Ann Landers, March 11, 1995.

It's in this kind of success, I believe, that genuine fulfillment lies. But success may mean something quite different to you.

Here's my suggestion: write a short essay—one typewritten page at most—that describes what you would consider success, what you want out of life, what you would find truly fulfilling.

You can either write it as a set of goals that you hope to accomplish before your life has ended, or as a make-believe obituary, self-composed.

If you choose to write your own definition of success, make it personal and specific—and prioritize. "I will consider myself a success if my children grow up to be happy and healthy, if my spouse and I grow old together, giving each other emotional, intellectual, physical, and spiritual pleasure. . . ." You fill in the rest.

If you choose to write your own obituary, talk first about what kind of man you were, what family, friends, and acquaintances thought of you, what impact you had on the lives of those around you. Save the résumé stuff for last.

When you're finished, I have some questions you might ask yourself:

1. Am I going in the right direction?
2. Am I concentrating on reaching these goals, or being that person?
3. If I'm not, why not? What's more important?
4. What am I waiting for?

I think you'll find there's a better way to live than by perpetuating the habits of your superman complex. I think you'll see you'll be better off storing your superman complex in the darkest, most distant corner of your mental attic.

Of course, you may worry about doing just that. You may ask yourself, "What will be left? Without my superman complex, just who am I?"

I'm about to tell you. . . .

Chapter Nine:

Without the Superman Complex, Who Are You?

Not long after I founded my consulting business, CRD, my superman complex suddenly went AWOL. Everything I touched turned to—well, not to gold, let me tell you. Business was so bad that I couldn't avoid serious self-doubt. Money-wise, we were down to the bottom of the barrel.

How terrible was it? Well, let me put it this way: at the time we lived in a fashionable Atlanta neighborhood, but the gas and water had been turned off because of non-payment. We were learning to live without such luxuries as folding money and credit cards.

One day, my wife was talking to a neighbor in our driveway when a tow truck pulled up. "Are you Susan Carey?" She naively said, "Yes, I am." The driver backed his tow truck into the driveway, attached his towing hitch to her car and towed it away. My wife, bless her, was up to the occasion. She turned to the neighbor, smiling, and said, "Oh, that Max. What a fun guy. He's always having surprise repairs done on my car!" She'd saved her pride—and mine—at least for a while.

It was during this period that I came to maintain the most accurate list in existence of Atlanta restaurants that didn't have electronic credit check machines, and didn't know that my American Express card wasn't working. I took Susan out to dinner that night—paying with my invalid American Express card—and we eventually started talking about our situation. At that moment, as you might guess, I was lower than low. I remember telling her, "I'm going to try to turn it around, but if I'm not good enough, we'll just have to learn to live with that."

Anyone who has the superman complex fears that just beneath it, behind the pretense and the posturing, the ambition and the hard work is . . . nothing. Or at least not much. Certainly not enough. Not enough to be proud of, or to impress others, or to accomplish anything noteworthy. I had that fear.

But one day, after all I'd been through, I was finally in the mood to find out the truth. I wanted to see if what I dreaded most was actually the case. Was I a hollow shell? A "suit"? A costume that walked and talked, with no fully formed human being inside, like Darth Vader? I asked myself this crucial question: how can I deal with reality if I don't know what it is?

I decided to find out, no holds barred, which I count as one of the most courageous acts of my life. I decided to look—*really* look—into the mirror. I decided to total up my assets and liabilities, entirely apart from what my superman complex was insisting they were.

I asked for help. In the end, I turned to lots of people at different times, in different ways, to different degrees—my wife, my minister, my best friend, a therapist. And I still do.

Then I began a process that hasn't stopped yet and I hope never will—a process I recommend strongly to anyone with a superman complex, because it is the only practical way we can overcome our doubts and start building a better, more balanced life. I gave each person permission to be honest with me—in fact, I pleaded with them (they didn't believe me at first).

I'm going to describe the process and how it works, so you can benefit from it yourself, or help someone else. But I'm not going to list *my* assets or liabilities—I don't want to do anything that could give my superman complex any ammunition. That's a joke, son.

Testing yourself

> *And all your future lies beneath your hat.*
> —John Oldham

I know how smart you *think* you are—but how smart are you really? How fast do you read and how much do you retain? Are you good at problem solving? How are your math skills? Do you write well? What's your reaction time? How little can you sleep and still function at the peak of your powers?

We've already established that people with the superman complex have a high opinion of all of their abilities. But I'm suggesting, as an antidote, that you test yourself and see how smart you really are.

Fortunately, it's not all that hard to find out what we're good at and what we're not so good at, to determine our innate skills, talents, and abilities. We can even do it in private, without help. How? Tests. Find the right aisle of your local library or bookstore—or check out booksellers on the Internet—and you'll discover armloads of books that will help you figure out your basic strengths and weaknesses.

The test books roughly fall into two categories: the ones that test your knowledge and the ones that test your abilities. A third, much smaller group, is aimed at helping you determine your preferences. Start with the aptitude tests, the ones designed to measure your raw abilities.

• Aptitude tests (or, are you really a Renaissance man?)

> *Knowing what you cannot do is more important than knowing what you can do. In fact, that's good taste.*
> —Lucille Ball

You'll find aptitude tests for every conceivable human quality. You can find out, if you're interested, whether you'd make a good mother-in-law, or a good dog trainer, or a good mail carrier. You may not care how you rank in these categories, but come to think of it, it wouldn't do you any harm to find out. Ability is ability and it's nice to know when you have it and when you don't. But if you're like me, you're interested in more substantial matters.

Find—and take—tests that measure qualities like these: reading speed and retention, computational ability, clerical skills, logical reasoning, spatial abilities, social proficiency, creative problem solving, mechanical aptitude, verbal fluency, and similar abilities. Take a couple of IQ tests as well.

Don't do this all at once, by the way. Spread the test-taking out over a few weeks, maybe a month. Otherwise, you'll get so sick of testing yourself you may throw up your hands at the whole idea.

Anyhow, when you're finished, take a long, objective look at your scores. Pretend you're looking at a stranger's results. My guess is that some scores will surprise you. Pleasantly in some cases, unpleasantly in others. You may discover you're terrific at doing something you've never even tried before—maybe someone with your spatial aptitude could be a first-rate architect. On the other hand, you may find that you have the verbal fluency of a mime. That would explain why you seize up when you sit down to write some kind of report.

Incidentally, you may have gone through this process before, or at least part of it. The Scholastic Aptitude Test has some similarities. Employment tests also try to quantify abilities, and not only abilities, but psychological strengths and weaknesses. But even if you've taken tests of this kind before, you may not know the results. Many people with the superman complex are their own bosses, so they've never taken employment tests, or the results have been confidential, or they're too high on the food chain to be subjected to indignities of this sort.

Anyhow, now, probably for the first time in your life, you know the truth about your abilities. Regardless of what your superman complex may tell you and the rest of the world, you can begin to know the reality behind the superman self-image.

- **Knowledge tests (or, deflating the know-it-all)**

OK, now the next part: what do you know, relatively speaking? If we listen exclusively to our superman complexes, we think we know just about everything, or at least everything that matters. Maybe so, maybe no. Think about the Internet, for example. Do you really know enough? I can tell you right now, I don't—but I'm learning. It may not even matter how much you know, exactly, but how much more you know than most people, or than anyone else. How you rate, I mean.

Go back to the library, the bookstore, or the Internet, or even better, a college bookstore. Get yourself an armload of tests. Try to cover all the fields that affect your life—business management, marketing, investing, accounting, government, the law, retirement planning, salesmanship, economics, information technology, finance, regulation, parenting, household budgeting, etc. You know your own list better than anyone else. But when in doubt, take that test too. Get it if it could conceivably have any meaningful application in your life or work.

Take all these tests over a period of time. Don't rush.

Don't wear out your test-taking gland. Just accumulate results. If you've chosen wisely, by the time you're finished, you should have a pretty good picture of where you're strong and where you're weak, whether you're at the top of your class, alone, or at the middle, or at the bottom with plenty of company.

• Preference tests (or, unburdening the glutton for punishment)

There's one more kind of test, optional but worth considering: the preference test. Preference tests are often given to high school seniors or college students to help them choose a career.

What kind of questions will you find on a preference test? Questions like these: would you rather tackle a difficult project alone or would you like experienced help? Do you prefer physical activities such as skiing or sedentary activities such as reading?

Of course, preference tests don't have any right or wrong answers. The only way to fail is to pull your punches, to shade your responses so you wind up with convenient results. If you answer the questions honestly, these tests will force you to *systematically* examine what you like and what you don't. Maybe you'll find you're already doing what makes you comfortable. But maybe you won't. And that's worth knowing.

Writing your private résumé

There's more to this "who are you" business than your abilities, knowledge and preferences. A human being's life and worth encompass much else, past and present—all of which must be included in any honest self-assessment.

> *Speak of me as I am. Nothing extenuate, nor set down aught in malice.*
> —William Shakespeare

Work life

Even if you've only been working for a few years, you probably have a longer list of accomplishments than you realize—and every one of them is an asset, because it's proof of what you can do.

I'm not talking here about titles, promotions, or salary levels. I'm talking about *actual* accomplishments: work done, triumphs, deadlines met, projects managed, reports written, goals met or exceeded, catastrophes overcome, competitors outwitted, battles won, duties discharged, disasters averted, unanticipated breakthroughs, surprise successes.

Make a list. Ask colleagues to jog your memory if necessary.

Next, make a list of those occasions where you fell short—forgetfulness, judgment errors, bad hires, missed opportunities, misinterpretations, misunderstandings, less-than-perfect performances. Don't leave anything off because of unusual circumstances, or because the blame wasn't completely yours. Be honest with yourself. After all, you won't be handing out this list to everyone you know. You're making it for your own private use.

What will you have when both lists are done? You'll have your *real* résumé. You'll be able to see, at a glance, what your genuine abilities are and where you don't quite measure up.

Add to this an examination of your relationship assets and liabilities. Your assets consist of your friends and supporters, both on the job and at other companies and organizations that affect your work life. Your liabilities include your enemies and opponents—people against you, not your ideas. They also include insincere supporters—yes-men, back-stabbers, and opportunists.

What's the purpose of all this? To make it harder—and also less necessary—to maintain the bogus self-image your superman complex tries to perpetuate, to give you a true picture of yourself. By the way, you don't have to write this down somewhere. But you should at least think it through. Be honest with yourself. You may be surprised by your conclusions.

Personal life

Now do the same thing for your personal life.

Consider your accomplishments and your failures: Have you provided well for your material needs and the needs of your family? Do you have a mutually satisfying and beneficial relationship with your spouse? Do you have good relationships with your children? Are you proud of the way they're turning out—or dismayed? Are you taking care of your health and your family's? Are you fulfilling your responsibilities to your parents and other relatives? Are you a good friend to your friends, new and old? Are you proud of your contributions to the community? If your mother knew everything, would she approve of the way you're living, morally, ethically, and legally?

The "yes" answers are your personal assets, the "no" answers are your personal liabilities.

Add to this an examination of your personal relationship assets and liabilities. Your assets consist of the people you can genuinely count as friends—not just acquaintances, but people you'd go out of your way to help and vice versa. Your liabilities include whomever you've wronged or mistreated or ignored and anyone else who dislikes you, for good reasons, bad reasons, or no reasons at all.

Another area filled with assets and liabilities: your personal activities. Hobbies are assets (and the lack of them, liabilities), so are interests (music, for instance, or politics or sports). If you have them, you have assets, because anything that broadens you and that expands your life is an asset. Other activities also count—jogging, churchgoing, attending a child's piano recital, going to the movies, bowling, playing tennis or golf (but not for work reasons).

In my opinion, a storehouse of good memories is an asset as well. But I can't say the same for bad memories, especially unresolved grief, frustrations, abuse (of you or by you), unhealed wounds, humiliations, and the like.

Same goes for personality traits. Are you calm, clear-headed, friendly, kind, generous, slow to anger, self-confident, relaxed, quick to laugh, forgiving, patient, optimistic? In our personal balance sheets, these are assets. And their opposites are liabilities: nervous, mean, easily enraged, frightened, tense, humorless, grudge-holding, etc.

Finally, you have physical assets—and liabilities. In any evaluation of yourself, these things matter also. Those of us with superman complexes tend to overestimate our physical abilities, especially our endurance. But maybe we can evaluate ourselves more accurately if we watch ourselves at play.

Here are some questions to ask yourself: How many sets of tennis am I comfortable playing in one day? How late am I willing to stay up to watch something on TV? When I'm on vacation, what do I eat, when do I eat, how long do I take? How fast do I read when I'm reading for pleasure? How fast do I walk when I'm not worried about being on time? How fast do I drive when the family is in the car and time isn't an issue?

Your answers to these questions are more likely to reflect your capability comfort levels than when your superman complex is cracking the whip.

To the extent your health is good, that's an asset. Illnesses or conditions are liabilities. Do you smoke? That's a liability. Are you overweight? Another liability. Are you getting old before your time, or still in your prime? Are you in good shape for your age? These factors also belong on your balance sheet.

If you think your way through all of this, or better yet, make yourself a balance sheet, you're going to have a pretty good idea of your strengths and weaknesses, no matter what your superman complex wants you—and the rest of the world—to believe.

Now that you know what you're truly capable of, it's time to consider the load you're carrying.

Responsibility inventory

> *Duties are not performed for duty's sake, but because their neglect would make the man uncomfortable.*
>
> —Mark Twain

What responsibilities are you carrying on your shoulders? Whatever they are, they're part of your total package, because they take a toll on your time, energy, and ability. What's left over, if anything, is what I call your psychic disposable income, the part of yourself you can spend on yourself or anything else you like.

Actually, your first responsibility is to yourself. "When the oxygen masks drop down, put yours on first, then help your child or the person next to you." If you don't take care of yourself, you can't take care of anyone else.

Of course, if you have the superman complex, you probably believe this doesn't apply to you. We superman types don't think we need much caring for, physically, psychologically, emotionally, even intellectually. We're just fine as we are and we always will be, because we're, well, superman.

But precisely because we're superman, we take on a mountain range of responsibilities, in a sense guaranteeing everyone in sight that they can depend on us, that we'll take care of things, and that no problem is too great for us to solve. We like people to be dependent on us—not independent.

Who's on your list?

- ***Family members***

Every adult feels—or should feel—responsible for his or her immediate family: spouse, children, often parents and sometimes in-laws. But those of us driven by our superman complexes frequently take on still more. We act like we are also responsible—parentally, as career advisors, as financial managers, as social directors—for our in-laws, our aunts, uncles and cousins, nephews and nieces, and all of their spouses and children.

- ***Work associates***

CEOs, company presidents, and others in command with the superman complex also tend to think they're at least somewhat responsible for the mental, physical, and financial well-being of colleagues, employees, stockholders, and other corporate stakeholders. Sometimes, these people number in the thousands. Don't tell me that responsibility isn't a burden, isn't draining. I know that it is, because I've felt it.

By the way, this especially applies to dangerous work. Like leading men into combat, or organizing a political protest, or working on a rescue mission, or helping shore up the dikes.

- ***The community***

We who have superman complexes are often not satisfied merely with taking responsibility for those who are close to us. Knowing how incredibly able we are, we are driven to do more. We chair the hospital fund drive. We coach Little League. We serve on the school board. "When you want something done, ask someone who's busy," the saying goes, and it could have been written to describe us.

- ***Our race, religion, and/or nation***

I'm a big Columbia football fan and an active alum. It's a wonder I don't rush out onto the field shouting "gimme the ball, gimme the ball," when the team is losing.

For superman-complex types like us, our responsibilities include every group we belong to. We stand ready to stick up for our team, school, branch of the service, race, religion, nation, or political party whenever it's under duress or needs our help. We're sure we can contribute something unique.

- ***Acts of God***

What do we think when it rains on the company picnic? We think it's our fault! We curse ourselves for not checking better weathermen in midweek. We fault ourselves for not choosing a different day, as someone has inevitably advised us. And we feel the same when the roof collapses, or we have a car accident, or the market falls, or the election goes wrong. When any of these things happens, we have a vague sense of failure. We've made a mistake of some kind. But that's not the problem. The problem is that—being a superman type—we're convinced that we control everything. The opposite is a lot closer to the truth.

All of the burdens we volunteer for out of an exaggerated belief in our abilities must be added to our personal balance sheets, as liabilities and not as assets. They are not based on reality and they are really designed to convince ourselves and others our abilities exceed normal human limits.

Help inventory

Fortunately, a counterweight exists to the burdens of

responsibility, if we superman types allow ourselves to accept it: outside help. Oddly enough, when you list sources of outside help, it looks a lot like the list of people we think we're responsible for. I'm sure there's a lesson in there somewhere, but I don't know what it is.

People with a superman complex are not inclined to ask for help. Think of a man pulling into a gas station and actually asking how to get someplace. But people who truly know their strengths and weaknesses also know when a little help might be all they need.

It's important for superman-complex types to learn to ask for help. It's one big way they can expand their capabilities and actually accomplish their inflated goals. It's a way of making up for whatever weaknesses we might have—the sort of weaknesses we've uncovered and hopefully admitted in our personal assessments.

In terms of that balance sheet we've been creating, every source of help is an asset. Here's a list of these assets, every one of which has the potential to make us stronger.

- ***Our spouses***

Who knows us better? Who can advise us more wisely? Who can point out our mistakes with more insight? Who can better offer emotional support? Whom are we more willing to listen to? I have no idea where I'd be today without the amazingly steadfast support of my wife when I needed it most. I haven't been able to thank Susan enough.

- ***Our children***

I know there are exceptions, but most of the time when we go to our children for help, we can be absolutely certain they're on our side. If they're old enough to understand our problems, they're probably old enough to offer advice. Also, they know and understand us well. And even if they can't help in the end, think of how they'll feel because you trusted them enough to ask.

- ***Our parents***

It's surprising how often older, wiser heads can contribute. Like our wives and children, our parents—in all likelihood—are on our side. They know our capabilities better than anyone else. What's more, they may have been where we are now, or someplace similar. Besides all that, helping us gives their lives meaning. By asking them for help, we're also giving them a present.

- ***Other relatives***

Got a big family? A truckload of uncles, aunts, and cousins? I know they can drive you crazy. But everyone has one good idea and they're all potential sources of free help, probably with a wide variety of knowledge and experience. Anyhow, it doesn't hurt to ask.

- ***Our friends***

What are friends for, if not to help and be helped? That's the whole idea. And when it works right, both people are stronger and happier, no matter which direction the help is going.

- ***Our work colleagues***

For those of us who are in high executive positions especially, our colleagues at work and our employees are excellent sources of help. Here is expertise, experience, talent, and creativity in quantity, available to us almost for the asking.

- ***Consultants and other experts***

What's the simplest course of action, if we don't personally have the expertise, knowledge, or skill that we need? Hire it. Go out and find the person you need—the best there is. Then honor his or her advice and help. Don't end up letting your superman complex take over, insist you know more than the expert and ignore the advice you've been given.

- ***Professional helpers***

If the help you need is not business-related, if it has to do with intangibles, such as troubled relationships, personal problems, matters of conscience, major life decisions, grief, psychological disturbances, and family emergencies, professional help is available. But all too often, people like us aren't willing to accept it. I'm talking about therapy and help from priests, pastors, rabbis, and ministers. We reject this kind of help because we think it makes us look weak. Actually, not accepting help is a sign of weakness. It's also a pretty poor way to solve problems.

- ***Total strangers***

The information society has given us a vast new source of help—total strangers. The Internet is filled with newsgroups, support groups, dedicated chat rooms—literally hundreds of places populated by anonymous people who, between them, have a storehouse of knowledge and experience equal to Harvard, the Menninger Clinic, the Louvre, and Sing Sing. You may have a bit of trouble separating the information from the disinformation, but probably not as much as you think. Intelligence and insight are just as obvious on the Internet as they are in real life.

> *When we turn to one another for counsel we reduce the number of our enemies.*
>
> —Kahlil Gibran

The real you

What do you have left when you strip away the superman complex, along with the carefully constructed self-image it perpetuates? Well, now you know.

We have strengths and weaknesses, assets and liabilities. We can't do everything, but we certainly can do some things. We can't control everyone and everybody, but we can manage ourselves, sometimes anyhow. We've also seen that we exist entirely apart from our accomplishments, and while work may take up much of our lives, there's more to life than work.

That was the purpose of this exercise—to prove that you've got a lot going for you even if you're not a superman, that even if you send your superman complex packing, there's plenty of you left. Who are we, without our superman complex? We are human beings, and that's not a fate worse than death.

Oddly enough, when we let our superman complex dominate our lives, we're actually less than we would be without it. In many ways, our superman complex prevents us from getting to some of the best parts of life—personal life and business life. There are goodies waiting for us when we're able to put our superman complex to rest. As you will soon see . . .

Chapter Ten:

What You Gain by Giving Up the Superman Complex

Sometimes I thank God for my early failures.

When we started CRD in 1981, it was a generic sales training company, pitted against a number of similar companies, most of them larger, better-established, with a more prestigious staff or glossier promotional materials. We were just too undercapitalized to compete for major deals with major companies.

Frankly, we were failing. And the funny thing is, impending failure is a terrific motivator. It inspires experiments and risk-taking. We'd noticed something strange in our sales training projects. Most of the people we were being asked to train were already pretty good salespeople. But they weren't meeting management's fairly reasonable goals. Why?

I took a chance. I called some of their prospects—not as a salesman, but as a researcher. I asked them how salespeople could improve their approach, how products or services could be better presented, how they could be better integrated into their prospects' needs.

When we started using this research in our sales training, the results were phenomenal. Sales *always* went up. This idea, born of impending failure, was soon giving us a reputation as a sales training company that produced amazing results. We started getting those once-elusive contracts. We followed up on that triumph by proposing to our clients' senior sales management that we use this approach to fine-tune the entire company's sales message. They loved the idea—and they were willing to pay for our research, which gave us a new profit vehicle.

Eventually, we were able to go to top management—CEO level—and say that we're changing the message of your sales force, we're changing your marketing message, we're even changing your product service message. Maybe, just maybe, we should be changing the message of your entire company, to align it with the needs and objectives of *your* clients.

Suddenly, we were a full-scale consulting firm. We had a new vision—to be the first company to not only create the marketing strategy or sales strategy, but also stay with the company through execution to ensure success.

As we evolved and broadened our services, we went from a company that had trouble landing a twenty-five-thousand-dollar contract to a company that could land one-year, multimillion-dollar contracts.

Failure—and the willingness to abandon a way of business that wasn't working—had done its magic. It had led us to a special place, a place we still occupy with great vigor. We had had the advantage of being disadvantaged.

Most people who have the superman complex are very reluctant to give it up, even though it is causing them to fail to find fulfillment in life. I include myself. We are comfortable, or so we tell ourselves, with the self-image we have created. We are comfortable telling ourselves and others that 1) we can do anything, 2) we're always right, 3) we don't need anyone, 4) we're in total control, 5) our work is our life, and 6) our achievements give us our identity. The six pillars of the superman complex give us aid and comfort.

We hold on to these behavior patterns, these ingrained habits, not because they are good for us—I think I've proved they're not—but because we are so familiar with them that we think they're us. But they're not us. They are patterns and habits that we've adopted, partly because they fit our inclinations, partly because of the way we've been raised, and partly because of the way we've reacted to social pressures.

But we can change. We can replace these habits with something better.

Here's the question: What do I *gain* if I put my superman complex in mothballs? How do I win?

If what's happened to me is in any way typical, someone who is able to overcome his or her superman complex will be showered with gifts that make life richer and more fulfilling. They follow one from another, almost inevitably.

Private life

> *The secret of life is enjoying the passage of time.*
> —James Taylor

When those of us with superman complexes are able to put them out to pasture, our private lives take on a new vitality, a new depth, a new joy. The reasons are many:

• To begin with, when our superman complex no longer rules our existence, we experience less stress, more energy, and a far greater ability to relax. We aren't squandering our psychic strength trying to be something we're not, in fact, something *nobody* is. We can take our eye *off* the ball for a change. We can let ourselves be distracted by something interesting.

• Because we're not forcing ourselves to work constantly, we have more disposable time to follow our interests, to spend time with people we like, to sit around and do absolutely nothing. We can go to the mall or the ballgame on a Saturday afternoon. And Sunday can truly be a day of rest. We can travel and leave our laptops and our cell phones at home. We can savor the present.

• We can be wrong from time to time without placing our identities at risk. Or, to put it another way, we can let other people be right. By "other people" I mean not only our spouses, our children, and our other friends and relatives, but also our colleagues. Don't they deserve a little time on the right side of a dispute? Don't they deserve to have their opinions respected and their judgments confirmed, at least occasionally? This is a gift we can give them when we stop trying to be a superman, when we can allow ourselves to be wrong occasionally.

• We don't have to bust a gut proving we can do *everything*. We can step aside and let others—friends or family—do what they do well, or well enough: choosing a restaurant, balancing the checkbook, cleaning out the garage, writing an essay for English I, training the dog, picking out the wallpaper—the list of things we *don't* have to do once we've kicked our superman complex out of the driver's seat is practically endless. And that means we can concentrate on doing what we're really good at, even if that means limiting our activities at home to taking out the trash, dozing on the couch, and pontificating about world events.

• We can actually *ask for help* when we need it. And we can admit that we need it. According to one school of belief, to which I happen to subscribe, helping each other is one of a family's core purposes. Someone who lets his or her superman complex dictate his actions, someone who sees himself as a Lone Ranger, short-circuits that function. He (or she) is actually stealing something from the rest of the family—the joy of helping him. But when he locks away his superman complex, he empowers his family and friends. He gives them the gift of trust.

• When we give our superman complex a one-way ticket to Timbuktu, we are relieved of the duty and burden of keeping everything and everyone under control, *our* control. We can let our children control their own lives, within reason of course. Likewise and even more so, our spouses. We can even, heaven forbid, let some things go completely. When I did that, I found to my amazement that no catastrophes came crashing down on my head. Nothing fell apart. All that really changed was my mood, which got a lot better.

• Without our superman complexes forever driving us on, preventing us from smelling the roses, our work is no longer our life. What is, then? Our life is our *life*—turkey dinner with the family, badminton in the backyard with the kids, walking in the woods, going to a ball game, talking—actually talking—with our spouses, sleeping late on a Saturday morning, taking in a concert, shopping, fixing a sticky door, meeting your daughter's new boyfriend—all the things life *should be about.*

• When we tame our superman complexes, and we no longer feel that we are our achievements and vice versa, who are we? We are some probably more interesting variation of the following: white, male, age forty-five, American, born in Ohio, Democrat, father, husband, son, pizza-lover, pick-up basketball player, stamp collector, nice guy, great talker, computer illiterate, NASCAR fan, admirer of Sharon Stone, dog lover, drinker of Miller Lite, believer in God, military vet, college grad, fairly smart fellow, slow to anger, unquenchable optimist, 42 regular, rather good looking, ten pounds overweight, in love with the wife, a snappy dresser—well, you get the idea. We no longer feel like phonies, fearing discovery.

Are our achievements still a part of us? Of course. But they're just another item in the list. In short, when we no longer get our identity from our achievements, we get it from who we really are. Even failure can't take that away from us.

We get many personal gifts when we get our superman complex under control:

> *Our lives teach us who we are.*
> —Salman Rushdie

- **The gift of self-knowledge**

Without a superman complex to constantly drive us, to help us avoid reflection and introspection, we can see ourselves for what we really are. We can take stock of ourselves objectively, as I've described in chapter 9. In my experience, when you're able to do that objective inventory, you'll be pretty pleased by what you find. You won't be superman, of course, not in reality. But you'll probably uncover some very real strengths you were only dimly aware of. And you will be relieved of the need for pretense. As for the weaknesses, when you identify them, you can compensate for them by asking for help, delegating, or sharing the work with people who are stronger in these areas.

- **The gift of genuine self-acceptance**

Everyone with the superman complex is, to some extent, rejecting who they really are in favor of who they think they have to be. But once we reject our superman complex, we can see ourselves for who we really are, discover we're okay after all.

When I became better at being who I truly am, I became better at what I did. I became a better entrepreneur, a better manager, and a better boss.

Self-acceptance, it turns out, is very relaxing. It relaxes other people, too. That's because it's the opposite of the characteristic striving of a person who has the superman complex. The energy released by self-acceptance, by knowing your strengths and your limitations and being satisfied anyhow lets you shift your focus from being someone you aren't to being exactly who you really are.

• The gift of empathy with other human beings

When we're in the grips of a superman complex, we have little if any feeling for other people's hopes and dreams and fears. We're much too busy singing our own song to hear any other music. But when we free ourselves of our superman complex, we cannot help seeing others more clearly as well . . . understanding them better . . . finding ways in which we're similar . . . identifying with them . . . and being able to share their joy and their pain.

Empathy is a quality people with the superman complex can achieve only superficially. They may learn the words, but they'll never be able to join the chorus.

What's good about empathy? If you really have it, people will trust you more. They will open up to you. It will help you understand that we're all in the same boat, that we have the same feelings, the same secrets, the same hopes and fears and, finally, the same human values.

> *True kindness presupposes the faculty of imagining as one's own the suffering and joys of others.*
>
> —André Gide

• The gift of feeling fully human

The odd thing about being superhuman is that when you feel that way, you're actually less human, not more. Nothing perfect is real. Real has imperfections, flaws, shortcomings. So do real human beings. So when we can give up being able to do anything, being always right, needing no help from anyone—ever, controlling everything and everyone, devoting our lives almost entirely to our work and depending on our achievements to give us identity . . . well, that's when we can start being fully human.

Being fully human comes with a number of penalties or drawbacks. When you're fully human, you risk failure, disappointment, discomfort, dissatisfaction, and tragedy. But only by taking these risks can you fully experience joy, triumph, success, comfort, fulfillment—and the rest of life's blessings.

When we give up our superman complexes, we get the gift of being real. It's hard to imagine a greater reward.

• The gift of a greater closeness with family and friends

What happens when we achieve real self-knowledge, when we learn to accept who we actually are, when we find ourselves feeling empathy with others, when we feel human, instead of like phonies—even to ourselves?

Well, I know what's happened to me and others like me who've managed to get their superman complexes under control. We've found ourselves with much deeper and more fulfilling relationships with our spouses, our children, our parents, and our other friends and relatives.

When we're playing our superman role, we are the captain of the ship, the commander of the brigade, the CEO of the family and its relationships with all of its friends. When we relinquish the role, we share authority. We share decisions. We share the load. We share ourselves. And our families will respond to our trust, our spontaneity, our authenticity, since that empowers them, helps them grow, and supports them. The result is a family atmosphere of greater support and affection and less anger and conflict.

• The gift of peace of mind

I am firmly convinced that, for people with a superman complex, the road to peace of mind begins with admitting that we have it and doing our very best to put it to sleep.

When we get our superman complex under control, we end the torture. We end the impossible pressure of trying to be perfect, to know everything. We end the agony of going through life feeling phony. We end the pressure of trying to live up to a self-image that is a lot more image than self. We end the strain of carrying the world around on our shoulders all by ourselves. We end the pressure of always having to live up to everyone's expectations.

If letting go of our superman complex had no other benefits, this would be enough in itself. But there are more. . . .

• The gift of a happier, healthier life

I don't know—for sure—if giving up your superman complex lengthens your life. All I have is anecdotal evidence based on my own experience and the experience of a few people I know.

But if stress, worry, pretense, impossible hours, ceaseless responsibility, and all the other pressures of trying to be superman take their toll on health—and I am sure they do—then letting go has to have a positive effect.

For those of us who have superman complexes, the benefits to our private lives of letting it go are priceless. And yet in some ways, the benefits to our business life—and to the companies we're involved with and the people we work with—may be even greater.

Business life

I'm sure that people with a superman complex can be found in every part of our society, and I suspect they're evenly distributed throughout the world. But nowhere are they more visible than in business and commerce, especially at the executive level. There, superman complex types are a glut on the market—and pose a serious problem. Companies are being led by people who aren't what they say they are, who aren't even what they think they are. As a result, companies must deal with all kinds of counter-productive executive behavior.

I know that corporations do benefit by employing driven people. In some ways, they get more than their money's worth out of employees who have some of the six pillars of the superman complex—workaholic, know-it-all, perfectionist control freaks. But the cost of their poor decisions, their mistreatment of people, their overarching ambition, their erratic management style saddle a company with poor results, high turnover, even failure and bankruptcy.

Can a CEO with a superman complex run his company if he lets go of the complex? I'm here to tell you he can. In fact, he can run it better, much better, both to his own benefit and his company's. And his colleagues' and his employees'.

When executives—like me—give their superman complexes the heave-ho, we become more productive, more fulfilled, and better managers. There are several reasons:

• We stop trying to do everything, which produces any number of excellent results: It relieves us of all kinds of burdens, especially the burden of accomplishing the impossible. It develops our delegation skills. It allows others to develop their talents, especially their executive talents. It demonstrates our trust in our colleagues and employees. It calls on underused corporate resources.

• We admit to the world that we make mistakes, at least occasionally. We no longer insist on our infallibility. This admission encourages a corporate culture where people take responsibility for learning. It encourages others to offer opinions and suggestions; it helps us be flexible enough to change course when it becomes clear we're on the wrong track; and it makes us more approachable and open to our colleagues and employees.

• We cease our intense efforts to be in control of everything and everybody. If that doesn't lower our blood pressure, I don't know what will. It's also likely to lower the blood pressure of those who work closely with us, because it returns to them something that shouldn't have been taken away in the first place: a sense of control over their work environments and their work habits. It allows them to feel like trusted adults, not erring children. The buck still stops at the top, but you create an empowered workforce.

• We stop trying to fill every waking moment with work. How does that help us on the job? It broadens us, exposes us to new ideas and people. It breaks our compulsive work habit patterns and encourages our creativity. It gives us more to bring to the job. It fills the gaps in our personalities. It makes us more interesting. It refreshes us. And for our colleagues, coworkers, and employees, it humanizes us. It helps us bond with them because we have more in common than work alone.

Some things don't get done, but they disappear by themselves because they really didn't need our attention anyway. Some things get done by other people, and better than if we had done them.

• We no longer depend on our achievements to give us identity. Among other things, that means we can take pleasure in the achievements of other people at our company. We can share the credit, or even give credit where credit is due. We can share the rewards with others who deserve them. We can contribute to our coworkers' self-esteem instead of tearing it down.

Stress reduced

The net result: when a corporate executive is able to fire his superman complex, he (or she) becomes a better manager of people and a less-stressed employee. He changes the working atmosphere for the people who work with him and, if he's high enough on the executive food chain, for the entire company.

Anyone who works for or with an executive who's shed his superman complex is likely to become a happier camper, a better team player, more likely to come in when he's feeling under the weather than take the day off, more likely to support his company's goals with action as well as lip service, less likely to check the want ads daily.

For the executives among us who are able to rise above our superman complex, the benefits both to ourselves and to our firms are many.

- ***Forward focus***

This means that we have a better idea of where to focus our efforts and where to get help by delegating critical tasks. It allows us to capitalize on our strengths and avoid attempting to slog through tasks we either hate or can't do well.

Along with a clearer view of our strengths and weaknesses, we get a clearer view of the strengths and weaknesses of those around us, because we're not blinded by our perfectionism, because we're not impelled to place blame, because we start from a position of respect, not contempt.

- ***Trust***

How do executives like us—minus our superman complex—change our behavior toward associates in ways that promote better relationships? We empathize with them. We recognize and respect their needs and fears. We treat them like fellow human beings. We criticize less and support more. We temper our demands. We don't get angry so easily. We don't insist on blaming. We compromise. We resist judging. We're less impatient. We can take a joke—and join in the laughter. The ultimate result—and reward? Mutual trust.

- ***Flexibility, resilience, skill***

When you're thundering along, full speed ahead, damn the fog, set on breaking a record, certain of yourself as a person can be, an unexpected iceberg dead ahead can be fatal. You know the story.

Well, that's the way life is for an executive with a superman complex—an unending series of high-speed runs through iceberg-infested waters, with no more guarantee of survival than just plain luck. High speed and determination aren't much good against the icebergs that can put a company at the bottom of the ocean: unexpected competition, labor problems, economic turndowns, supply problems, product safety defects, and the other assorted horsemen of the corporate apocalypse.

But when an executive like me puts his superman complex away, he's no longer driven by his need to succeed, his conviction that he's right, his inability to accept help, his urge to control everything. The only thing that drives him is good sense and talent. If the business situation changes, that man doesn't have to prove he was right anyhow. He doesn't have to forge ahead regardless. He can adjust. He can get advice. He can reassess the situation. He can compromise. He can roll with the punches and land on his feet.

What I'm saying is that if you're an executive with a superman complex—like me—there is a treasure trove of gifts awaiting you. You can have a richer, more fulfilling life, you can be a better manager, better husband, better father, if only you will change.

You know that old joke, "How many psychiatrists does it take to change a lightbulb?"

Answer: "Only one, but it takes a long time and it has to *want* to change."

Chapter Eleven:
Making Changes

> *Change is not made without inconvenience, even from worse to better.*
>
> —Richard Hooker

Not long ago, I gave a speech at a luncheon for entrepreneurs. I brought one of my associates along and afterward, she sat a few seats away from me at the luncheon table. After a while, I realized that the woman sitting next to her was talking to her with unusual earnestness. Curious about what she might be saying, I unobtrusively tuned into the conversation.

The other woman was telling my associate about her boss. "He's so dogmatic," she complained, "so single-minded, so tunnel-visioned. He has to be in control of everything."

"I understand," my associate said, "I truly do. My boss, Max, used to be that way too."

Used to be. I've never gotten more pleasure from a bit of eavesdropping. It made me feel that I had genuinely changed, and that maybe I could turn my attention from myself to growing my company and fully leveraging the talents of those around me. My associate didn't realize it, but she had given me a great gift.

The "gift"

As you may have gathered in reading the previous chapter, one of my favorite ideas—and a theme in many of my speeches—is this concept of "the gift." I'm not talking about presents people give you. I'm talking about the blessing hidden in every frustration, every setback, and every failure, if you're willing to look for it. It's a concept that I learned from a good friend and fellow pilot, a fellow named Pat Moneymaker. "Max," he always used to say, "when one door closes, another door opens. Look for the gift. Look for the gift."

I had first discovered the profound truth of those words early in my business career after I had been working at Ryan and Associates for a few years and had come to a dead end.

I'd been moving up the ladder steadily, driving myself to overcome every challenge. Racking up successes, promotions, and recognition. And thanks to my superman complex, I'd convinced myself that every time I overcame a new challenge, I was "growing." In fact, I was standing still.

In a way, accomplishments, praise, and rewards are like candy bars. They taste great. They even energize you. But you quickly forget the taste and the energy is only a sugar high. So you're always seeking another fix. When I was out in the field, putting out fires, charging up a sales force, bringing in the numbers, I was getting a steady stream of fixes.

Then I got myself into a situation where the fixes came to a crashing stop. I got promoted to the head office in Chicago. I was now, officially, part of the inner circle—a "made man," as the Mafia says. My salary jumped several levels. I was enrolled in a weekend executive MBA program at the University of Chicago, and everybody made it abundantly clear to me that from this point on in my career, I was on the ultimate fast track.

I should have been thrilled, right? After all, this is what I'd been working for like crazy for the past six years. But once the initial euphoria faded, I soon found I wasn't getting the achievement fixes I needed. I wasn't running my own show anymore. I wasn't facing a stream of constant challenges. I was mired in the bureaucracy and not making much of a difference on a day-to-day basis. I was, well, I was unsatisfied, even bored. I wanted to be on the front lines, not in the back room. I was suffering acute withdrawal.

I discussed my dissatisfactions with a Ryan coworker who was feeling much the same way. We decided that the only way to get the action we craved was to start our own business. I immediately reported my decision to my manager, assuming that he and the rest of the top executives would support me, recognize my years of contributions, and wish me well. A rousing "going-away" party would not have been out of the question.

In fact, there was no send-off party, no round of handshakes, no "We'll miss you but . . ." speeches. What happened instead? My manager (who'd been loudly singing my praises until then) berated me for better than a half hour, telling me (1) I wasn't nearly the hotshot I thought I was; (2) I had absolutely no chance of being successful on my own; and (3) once I walked out the door, they would never take me back. So much for the farewell cake.

But what's important about this story is not so much what my manager said to me that day. It's how I reacted. Not once during his tirade did I try to defend myself. I didn't stand up, pound my fist on the table, and say, "Whoa, I know you're upset, and I know I owe this company a lot, but come on. This is getting out of hand." Even worse, I walked around the rest of that weekend in a catatonic daze. Me, Mr. Bounceback, Mr. Resilience, Mr. Top-Gun Navy Pilot.

That thirty-minute conversation swept away all the ego strength that I had presumably accumulated during all those years of success and recognition at Ryan, not to mention all my other achievements since age five. Talk about a wake-up call.

That Saturday, I was a zombie. Sunday morning, still in bed, I reached into the nightstand, hoping to find a book I could hide in. One book, a paperback, tumbled onto the floor beside me and landed on the carpet, open, with two pages of print staring up at me.

The book was *Your Erroneous Zones*, by a psychologist named Wayne Dyer. It was a huge bestseller in the early 1970s. I still don't remember how this book had ever come into our possession, but there it was. And as I bent over to pick it up, I couldn't help reading the chapter title on the open page: "You Don't Need Their Approval," it said.

There's a wonderful scene in the Robert Redford movie *The Natural* where at the exact moment that he hits a game-winning home run in the pennant playoff, lightning strikes the light towers, which burst out into a dazzling fireworks display of popping bulbs while Redford runs around the bases.

No, lighting didn't strike that morning when I looked down at the book on the floor and saw that chapter headline, but I will tell you this much: those words gave me a heck of a jolt.

I read the chapter—or, more accurately, I devoured the chapter, as though it was a canteen of fresh water and I hadn't had a drop to drink for three days. And nearly everything that Dyer had to say in the chapter was exactly what I needed to hear.

Yes, I had received a gift. A door had been opened. And again, later in my business life, when I was on the verge of failure, when I had my near breakdown on the deck, I found another door.

Hoping to find some peace, I'd begun meeting in private with another Vietnam vet, who had problems similar to mine. He'd dealt with them by getting involved in vet activities and getting some therapy. The combination, he told me, had helped him begin to heal, to tame some of his demons, to take back control of his life.

Therapy didn't appeal to me. My superman complex was still insisting I didn't need help, especially not from a stranger who hardly knew me. How could he figure out what was wrong and how to fix it?

Then came the miracle, which is not a word I use lightly. I ran into Alan Yorker, a classmate at Columbia—and a psychotherapist. And pretty soon, I found myself dropping in on him from time to time, talking things over with an old friend. Well, that's how I described it to myself. That I could deal with.

Alan quickly allayed my fear that I was going "crazy." He agreed that some of what I was going through was connected to the grief and fear of Vietnam experiences I hadn't come to grips with. But he also got me to see there was much more to my troubles than that.

Simply put, I was starting to run out of psychological energy. I thought I'd been handling the pressures and stresses of keeping my business afloat quite well. But that was my superman complex talking. I was really fooling myself. Alan helped me realize I'd been stuffing my conflicts and problems into my subconscious rather than confronting them and resolving them. This is classic superman-complex-type behavior. You don't acknowledge your fears or allow your emotions to surface: you keep everything buried. Unfortunately, hiding your feelings from yourself takes a serious amount of energy and the only payoff is that you become more and more disconnected with your true self.

Take the conflict you experience in war—not the terror of risking your life, but the fact that you are *expected* to kill people, you get *rewarded* for it, and you get punished for *not* doing it. And you're not always sure of *why* you're doing it. You're trying to kill total strangers, living in places you've even never heard of.

These actions are in conflict with everything you've been taught so far in life. Yes, I know we see violence on TV and in the movies, but our basic teaching remains: violence is wrong and killing is the very worst kind of violence. How do we deal with contradictions like this? We bury them deep in our subconscious. And we spend a lot of energy keeping them buried. This was the very energy I needed to deal with the everyday stresses of business. And when I ran short, I started to fall apart.

I was lucky. I'd gotten myself so deeply in trouble that I'd had to seek help. If the stress hadn't overwhelmed me, I might have limped along for a long time, pretending I was superman, until the inevitable crash. That crash never came, thanks to Alan, to my wife, and a lot of other people who helped me during this difficult period. I was able to start digging up my conflicts and dealing with them, bit by bit. But it took time.

Typically—and ironically—as soon as the crying jags eased and I realized I wasn't going crazy, I fell back into my old pattern. Identify the problem. Figure out a plan. Make it happen. A superman at work.

Alan stopped me. He showed me how I was only hurting myself with my arbitrary single-minded attempts to control my business, my employees, my family, and everyone else in my life. Without ever using the phrase "superman complex," he got me to see—for the first time in my life, really—that *my* way of overcoming adversity may not have been the only way, or, for that matter, the "best" way. He got me to see the gap between my self-image and who I really was.

"Let me guess what it's like in your company," he said in one memorable conversation. "The people are detached, they're a little afraid of you, and they do what you tell them to do, and that's about it. You feel they're not contributing."

I told Alan that he was absolutely right, but, keeping in character, I added, "What's wrong with them?"

"Max," Alan said. "The question is what's wrong with you."

Now, finally, I realized that something had to change . . . and that something was me.

For many people, change is one of the most terrifying words in the English language. It means giving up the familiar in exchange for the strange and new. "Better the Devil you know than the Devil you don't," we say.

And as for *personal* change, well, even when life is bad, even when we know we should change, even when we know we're shortchanging ourselves and everyone we know simply by being the way we are, we resist changing with every fiber in our bodies.

Barriers to change

Why, for God's sake? Why in the world do we resist change with such determination—even when we *know* we should change?

We don't think we *can* change

The first reason we resist change is that we're afraid we can't. We're afraid we're stuck with the way we are. "I am who I am," as Popeye said, meaning take or leave it, he wasn't changing, he couldn't change. He was born that way. And how can you change if you're born that way? "Can a leopard change its spots?"

Well, as I've discussed in chapter 5, the superman complex has a combination of causes. Yes, one of them is genetic, and there's no changing that component, not yet anyhow. Upbringing is another component that's pretty hard to change as long as time travel is beyond us. And there's not an awful lot we can do about the social pressures that make people want to act like supermen.

But I am utterly convinced that while we may be genetically *inclined* toward a superman complex, while our parents might have pushed us in that direction, while we may have been influenced by social pressures, our superman complex is mainly a very well established set of *habits*. And habits can be broken.

We fear we'll lose our identities

> *Identity would seem to be the garment with which one covers the nakedness of the self.*
> —James Baldwin

The second reason is that we're afraid of what would happen if we *did* manage to change. We're afraid we'd lose our identity—the identity we depend on. We're afraid that if we give up our self-image we'll be left with no image at all. We don't know who or what we'd be.

If we give up our superman complex, we fear, maybe we'd lose all of our drive and ambition. If we started to empathize with others, maybe we'd lose our ability to command. If we saw ourselves as nothing more than human, and not that superhuman tower of strength we presented to the world, maybe we'd fall apart.

The truth is, sidetracking our superman complex is not the same as a frontal lobotomy. It doesn't subtract anything real. It adds something: a layer of awareness and understanding, and ability to see yourself better—both making it harder to ignore the way you're acting . . . and the way you're feeling.

For me, putting my superman complex aside has made me more productive and more successful. It has improved my judgment. It's made me a better manager. It's given me more energy and more time. It's improved my relationships with people.

But it hasn't taken my identity away from me. If anything, it's made me more of what I really am. It's made me better than I was. But I'm still the same old Max. In fact, I'm still the same old Billy Carey.

We're comfortable the way we are

> *The lust for comfort, that stealthy thing that enters the house a guest, and then becomes a host, and then a master.*
>
> —Kahlil Gibran

The third reason we're reluctant to change is that regardless of the problems we're causing ourselves and others, we're comfortable the way we are. Or at least comfortable enough. We've always been this way and it's worked. But has it really? Will it continue to?

You know the old saying about the employee who was too bad to keep but too good to fire? That's our superman complex. Ambition, determination, the willingness to work hard, to take on responsibility—all of those are, after all, good qualities. In moderation.

Comfort is dangerous. It slows your thinking. It makes you lazy—not about your work, but about yourself. It is deceptive, because it makes you think everything is just fine. Comfort is a kind of rationalization. When you're comfortable, you say, "Why change?" "Why look at myself more closely?" "Why challenge myself?"

Comfort leads to complacency, complacency leads to stagnation, stagnation is the end of growth. That's why I say it's dangerous.

We're not quite ready. . . .

The fourth reason we're reluctant to change: we have unfinished business, goals not yet met, achievements not yet completed. Someday, we'll get to it, someday we'll take the plunge and maybe give up that ol' superman complex.

Just not today. And by the way, not tomorrow either.

Delay seems like a way of saying yes and no at the same time. Actually, it's just a wimpy way to say no. It's a way to put off saying yes until another time, and when that time arrives, putting it off again and again until everyone, including you, forgets about the whole thing.

When I was in high school, I found myself thrown together with a very pretty girl who was much more sophisticated than I was. I was desperate to look cool. And, having the gift of gab, I was doing pretty well—until she opened her purse, took out a pack of cigarettes and offered me one. I didn't smoke—I'd tried cigarettes and gagged. But I couldn't tell her I didn't smoke. It would have made me look like a twelve-year-old.

I waited for what seemed like fifteen minutes but was probably more like fifteen seconds for my brain and my mouth to get together and find a way out of the predicament. To my amazement, they did. "Not now," I heard myself saying. "Oh," said the girl, thinking nothing of it, "okay."

Since then, "not now" has gotten me out of a number of problems. But it's also gotten me into trouble, by letting me put off something I should be facing immediately. So when I hear myself saying "not now" these days, I ask myself what's really going on.

People are depending on us

Reason five for not changing: people are depending on us to be the way we are. They're depending on us to tell them what to wear, to dominate any meeting, to approve or disapprove of their plans, to pick up the slack when others tire, to issue orders, to make sure things are done right. That's the way we see it anyhow.

The way we see it, we are indispensable. It's not our fault, it's just the way things are. Without us, the family, the company, the enterprise, the effort will collapse. So we simply *have* to be superhuman. It's our duty, our responsibility, our burdensome lot in life.

The fact is, though, that when indispensable people depart the scene, life goes on. They are replaced, sometimes by people not as good, sometimes by better people. So in my opinion, when someone tells himself he's indispensable, he's usually not making an objective evaluation, just letting his ego off the leash.

Will your world collapse if you cease being superman? Not likely. You won't be boxing up your knowledge and talent and storing it away in the attic. You'll simply be playing to your strengths and giving others a chance to help you where you need it. You'll be sharing command. You'll be allowing others to be right on occasion. You'll be mixing a little fun in with all that work.

By the way, I didn't learn about all this in a psychology book. I've lived every bit of it. I've felt the sheer terror of committing myself to change. I've felt I was sailing toward the edge of the world, closing in on the territory marked "there be monsters here" on ancient maps. And I'm still here, better than ever by most accounts.

We're simply . . . afraid

> *Do that which you fear the most and the death of fear is certain.*
>
> —Aristotle

Finally, we avoid change because the whole idea just . . . scares us.

On the football field, in the air over Vietnam, in clients' offices, and my own boardroom, I think I've learned a little about fear. The most important thing I've learned about it is that it is very useful. I say, listen to your fear. Your fear helps you set priorities. It points directly at something you should be working on—something you desperately want to avoid, but shouldn't.

Your fear also tells you what you don't know. The fear signals go up the moment you reach unknown territory. How to put them away? Go exploring. Take the risk. Get to know the territory.

When you overcome your fear, you get a great gift: you get self-confidence. You learn that you can survive, even thrive, despite your fears.

How Much Change?

When people talk about changing themselves—or someone else—they're usually referring to major alterations, not a nip here and a tuck there. Well, I'm not. I'm talking about a new paint job, not an engine replacement. I'm talking about a shift, not a transformation.

Frankly, I'm not much of a believer in transformation. We've all spent years becoming who we are and a lot of that was built in to begin with. But we can learn to lead with our left instead of our right. We can learn to pump the brakes instead of slamming them to the floor. We can learn to look before we leap.

I know how frightening change is, how challenging a task. I know that it is the ultimate uphill battle. But I also believe completely that it's possible for practically everyone. Heck, if I can do it . . .

So, dear reader: here's your challenge. Up periscope, take aim, fire your torpedoes, and send that damnable superman complex to the bottom. Make your own personal ocean safe for the real you to lift anchor, leave port, and cruise around in any likely direction.

Actually, I'd like to direct that challenge not to the PT boat within you, but to the submarine—to your superman complex, that is. I want you to make this your superman complex's final task, taken on with your usual workaholic, know-it-all, perfectionist, control-freak determination. In short, I want you to give it all you got.

Yes, but *how?*

Techniques for changing

> *It is easier to sail many thousand miles through cold and storm and cannibals, in a government ship, with five hundred men and boys to assist one, than it is to explore the private sea, the Atlantic and Pacific Ocean of one's being alone.*
>
> —Henry David Thoreau

Changing is really just a special kind of learning. It's learning to stop doing one thing and start doing another instead. And learning is as natural as breathing.

Nonetheless, I think it's easier if you take it step by step. So here are the steps, as I see them:

1. Be clear about what you want to change

If the train's on the wrong track, it doesn't matter how fast it goes—it will never get to its destination. Same with making alterations in your character and personality. Remember the old tailor's warning: "Measure twice, cut once."

By now, it should be pretty clear what needs cutting, for those of us with a superman complex. It's those six pillars I described earlier:

- *The Renaissance man (I can do anything)*
- *The know-it-all (I'm an expert at everything)*
- *The glutton for punishment (I can work 24/7)*
- *The Lone Ranger (I need no help or advice)*
- *The puppet master (OK, so I'm a control freak)*
- *The hall-of-famer (Reward me over and over again)*

Remember, some of these personality traits will play a greater role in your life than others. No one will know better than you which apply to you and to what degree. So this is the time for some self-reflection. That's job number one.

2. Make a contract with yourself

Once you have a clear picture of your particular superman complex, it's time to take the next step: committing yourself to boxing it up and putting it into cold storage. I think you should do that in a concrete way. It shouldn't simply be another New Year's resolution, but something more formal, more ceremonial. What I have in mind is a written contract with yourself, something more tangible, more real than a silent promise. Here's how it could look:

> *I, Max Carey, recognizing that I have a superman complex, do hereby promise myself, my family, my friends, and the people I work with that I will do my utmost to break the habits that characterize the condition: acting like I think I can do everything and that I know everything, working every available moment, seldom asking for help or advice, being a control freak, and seeking glory or reward at every opportunity. I make this solemn pledge because I am convinced that it is the clearest, shortest, surest path to a happier, healthier,*

and more fulfilling life, not only for myself, but for the other important people in my life.

This formal commitment to yourself should be just the beginning, in my view. In a way, abandoning your superman complex is like quitting cigarettes: the more public you make your promise, the more you empower others to help you, the better chance you'll succeed. Start with those people you care about most.

3. Go to your family

Except for ourselves, no one is more affected by our superman complexes than our spouses, our children, our parents, and other close family members. They have to deal daily with our tempers, our absences, our domination, our emotional distance, our micromanagement of everything and everyone we can see or touch. They pay the price for our behavior, our bad habits.

Nothing could be more fitting, then, to involve them in our pledge to change. If we succeed, they will be the most prominent beneficiaries. If we fail, they'll suffer. Furthermore, at least in some ways, they know us better, they see us more clearly, than we do ourselves.

But it is not enough to promise them we'll change, no matter how serious we are or say we are. We have to put our money where our mouth is, we have to practice—from this moment on—what we're preaching in our contract with ourselves.

How? By giving our family members permission to point out—nicely and kindly, thank you—when we're slipping into the very habits we're trying to change, by *asking* for their help, by trusting our family with our awareness and understanding of ourselves. I'm not talking about a scene comparable to the reading of your father's last will and testament. I'm talking about an intimate sharing of feelings, a moment of high affection and trust, and most importantly, a time of *laughter.*

After all, a lot of superman-complex behavior is very

funny, if you look at it from the right point of view. Think about it: we can do anything? We know everything? We can work harder, faster, smarter than anyone else? We have some kind of divine right to control everything and everyone we can? If we came across someone else who claimed all these qualities, we'd have a pretty good chuckle about it, right? So why not laugh when we present ourselves as omnipotent, all-knowing, and superhuman? And why not let others laugh too?

If we laugh at ourselves when we insist we're superhuman and let others laugh with us, the behavior will deflate like a punctured balloon. We'll rob it of the pomposity it needs in order to survive. Eventually, we won't be able to act that way anymore without cracking a rueful grin.

So, outside of laughter when we're acting ridiculous, what kind of help do we need from our family? What should we ask them for? Gentle, affectionate, but persistent reminders, I think. Here are some examples of what I mean, along with some appropriate responses we can make:

Spouse: "Nick's sleeping over at Neal's tonight. Why don't we just . . . stay home and cuddle up with some popcorn and an old movie?"

You: "That's a wonderful idea, sweetheart. I assume you want me to rent *An Affair to Remember* again?"

Son: "Dad, you promised you wouldn't work Saturday morning—that you'd go to my basketball game."

You: "You're absolutely right. Let's go. You want me to pick up some tape for the video camera?"

Spouse: "You've chosen our vacation destination the last five years. I think it's my turn, don't you?"

You: "Yes it is. Why don't you decide on a place and make it a surprise? All I ask is that you pick a destination we can get to using our frequent-flyer miles."

Daughter: "My teacher told me to do it *this* way, Dad."

You: "Well, do it the way she said. She's the one who gives you your grade."

Spouse: "There's a gas station up there. They'll know where Elm Street is."

You: "OK, I'll pull in there and I'll ask. Wanna come along and take notes?"

Your mother: "Why don't you come here for Thanksgiving this year? We'll get the whole family together."

You: "Sounds great. It's been too long since we've all seen each other. Tell everyone I'm really looking forward to it. Tell them I actually mean that."

Daughter: "You don't need to shout, Dad."
You: "I know. I'm sorry. I'll whisper instead."

Son: "I know the garage still isn't *perfectly* clean, Dad. But I think it looks pretty good."

You: "You're right. Good job. Let's go out and get some ice cream."

Spouse: "Don't you think we should call a plumber this time, dear?"

You: "Absolutely. I think I proved my incompetence last time."

Get the idea? Our families have a stake in our shedding our superman complex. If we genuinely ask for their help, chances are they'll be very happy to give it. And they'll be even happier if we respond positively—and with a sense of humor.

4. Talk to your friends

> *Some people go to priests; others to poetry; I to my friends.*
> —Virginia Woolf

After we've gotten things on track with our family, it's time to do the same with our friends. My suggestion is that instead of telling them what's on our minds one at a time, we get them together, maybe for a barbecue or a golf game. We can say we have a story we'd like to share with them, something important. You'll do it your own way, I know, but you could start out like this:

"I've been taking a look at myself and the way I work and live, and I've come to some conclusions I'd like to share with you. This probably isn't going to come as a surprise to you, but I think I've been having some problems with what's called 'a superman complex.'"

Then we tell them what the superman complex is and how we fit the description. Tell them what we've decided to do about all this—and about the agreement we've made with our family. Do it with humor.

Finally, we should enlist their help, for our friends, like our family, have often seen us in superman-complex mode, to their dismay, and they'll relish the idea of helping us cut this sort of behavior out of our repertoire.

What kind of help do we want? Exactly the sort we've asked our family to provide: firm but gentle reminders when we're working too hard, claiming we're omniscient, making all available decisions, rejecting needed help or useful advice, producing everything from dinner on the town to the weekly poker game, all the while keeping our emotional distance from everyone.

We need this help because our superman-complex habits are so ingrained that we have trouble seeing them. We're like the basketball player in the locker room after the big game who says, "Odor? What odor?" We need objective noses to sniff out our own superman complexes.

5. Discuss it at work

No, I'm not suggesting you write an editorial in the company newspaper about your superman complex and charge every employee with notifying you every time they see you violating your oath to stop being superman.

What I am suggesting is that you gather your closest work associates and tell them what's up. Give them the same rap, more or less, that you gave your friends, adjusted for the work scene. It might help if you pointed out examples of the kind of behavior you're talking about—recent examples of your own actions at work: killing a messenger, demanding harder work or longer hours than Scrooge required of Bob Cratchit, trying to do everything yourself, assuming no one else knows how to do anything except you, taking credit for everything, demanding from employees the kind of respect normally reserved for kings, constantly criticizing or blaming your colleagues and subordinates.

Make it clear that you really want to change and you can use their help: a quiet word when they see you transgressing on your own good intentions. You're not looking for a barrage of criticism, you don't want your authority undermined, but you're ready to give up your bad behavior and you're ready to admit you're human—not superhuman. You're ready to start laughing at yourself—and let them do the same when it's appropriate.

You should also share with your work associates the reasons you want to change, which are strikingly simple and hard to dispute: to live a happier, healthier, more fulfilling life and to act in a way that helps others do the same.

Why am I suggesting that people with the superman complex go public when they want to defeat it? Well, I'm upping the ante. It's the same philosophy behind the idea of big weddings. Make stakeholders out of the community, so they'll help you succeed.

6. Take it in stages

If you keep in the forefront of your mind the idea that you're engaged in a total transformation, that you're changing all kinds of characteristics, you're likely to fail. You have to do it in stages, small stages.

But which part of your superman complex do you take on first? That depends on your style. Some people like to tackle the toughest work first. If they can do that, they tell themselves, the rest will come easily. Fair enough. But some people like to work on the easiest jobs first. That way, by the time they get to the hardest ones, they have the work mostly finished and they can concentrate their entire energy climbing that last mountain. That's fine too.

I think this is a matter of personal styles. You probably know your style quite well. Stick with it. Do what's comfortable for you. But take the offending traits one at a time. Think about a single personality trait that badly needs to be taken down a few pegs—the workaholic in you, for instance. Think about how you spend the day, how you spend the week, how you spend the weekend. Think of your vacations—how frequent, how long, what kind, what you remember about them, how you feel about them.

Ask yourself at what exact moment does the workaholic within you assert itself. "Won't be home for dinner tonight, honey." "I have some work to do this weekend. Why don't you take some photos at the recital?" "If I leave for my business trip Sunday night instead of Monday morning, I can get an early start on Monday."

Your job: to become painfully aware of each moment your workaholic self kicks in, then stomp on it. Decide to do the opposite. Consciously and with determination. Don't go down to your office. Don't work late. Don't catch the Sunday night red-eye that will not only get you to your Monday morning appointments early but will prevent you from spending an evening with your family.

And altering the pattern once won't do. You must spot the decisive moment time and time again and forbid yourself, on pain of self-contempt, from making the usual choice. You must substitute a conscious choice not to work overtime for the automatic decision to keep working. And you must do that again and again until the automatic decision is to stop working. If you're vigilant and consistent, you'll vanquish the workaholic within you in a few weeks.

When you've beaten this bad habit, it's time to take on another aspect of your superman complex. The next hardest? The next easiest? Your choice. But don't forget: if the first habit shows up again—and it will, believe me—clobber it again and again, until it's just a memory.

Chapter Twelve:

Habits to Break, Habits to Make

Back in the days when I was just starting as a combat pilot, I was a Lone Ranger. Early on in my Vietnam tour, though, my squadron commander and wingman—who flew beside me during combat missions—broke me of that superman-complex habit.

It takes more than one pair of eyes to win a dogfight. When you're flying combat, your wingman, the pilot in the plane next to yours, is the most important person in the world. He's there to warn you when there's danger at your six o'clock—directly behind you. He's there to bring you back safely when you get into trouble. Usually, the squadron commander acts as wingman to the newest, greenest pilot in the squadron, to keep him alive until he can do what's required. In my case, I was lucky that my squadron commander (and wingman) was one of the best pilots in the Navy—a former Blue Angel.

I was so cocky that I became careless. I got into the habit of not paying attention during the pre-flight briefings. The fact that I was part of a *team*, and that I had a responsibility to my teammates somehow escaped me.

One afternoon on a routine mission, both of us, the skipper and I, had just launched from the ship and were getting ready to rendezvous in preparation for our flight route to the Vietnam coast. I was all set to tuck myself under his wing when I saw him making furious hand signals: tapping his index finger against his helmet and then making the thumbs-down sign. I got the message: his radio wasn't working.

At first, I was relieved. I thought this meant we'd abort the mission and head back to the ship. No combat that day. But the commander had a different agenda—or so he indicated by his *next* set of hand signals. He tapped the front of his helmet and pointed to me. I got the message: the mission was going to go on, dead radio or not, and *I* was going to lead it. Relief turned to alarm, then terror.

I had to figure out where we were going—pronto. I unfolded a huge, unwieldy map, frantically setting the navigational fixes, adjusting the radar, running down radio checkpoints—all the while struggling to keep my voice calm when I checked with the other pilots, to hide my panic and confusion.

Though I finally managed to get us to the beach and back, it was a nightmare. As we headed back to the ship, I was bone weary and soaking wet from all the tension—and the worst was yet to come. Because the skipper's radio wasn't working, he couldn't get any instructions from the ship. It was up to me to guide him all the way back to land on the ship, with the instructions I was getting on *my* radio.

At best, this maneuver is about half an inch away from impossible. First, you have to fly close enough to the other plane so that the pilot can see you. Then, you have to get into a holding pattern, call the ship, and get a time when you can come down. After that you have go through a very precise route, with the other plane close enough so that you can use hand signals to tell the pilot when he should lower his gear and flaps, to make sure he's okay, and to take him all the way to the so-called "meatball"—the electronic landing signal—on the deck. There is very little margin for error, because you're so close to each other and the ship.

When you're done and he's about to land, you give

him the "kiss off"—hands to your mouth, fingers against your lips, then the kiss. It's a loving gesture: it says, "You're on your own." And when I did that, I heard my skipper's voice, loud and clear, in my earphones seconds later. "Thanks, Max," he said. "Nice job."

You guessed it. I'd been set up. His radio had been working just fine from the start. What *wasn't* working, in his judgment, was *me*. He had been watching me closely, particularly during the pre-flight briefings, and he realized I was getting slack—putting us both in danger.

I got the message loud and clear. Bad habits can kill you. I broke myself not only of the habit of letting my mind wander during briefings, but of the superman attitude that I didn't have to perform for the good of the entire squadron. In business, this translates to take care of your teammates, so you will earn and deserve their trust.

I didn't know it at the time, but later I realized that I would have a lot of bad habits to break, habits I didn't even know were habits, because they seemed so much a part of me.

Separating you from your bad habits

> *Habit is habit, and not to be flung out of the window by any man, but coaxed downstairs a step at a time.*
>
> —Mark Twain

Maybe your genes predispose you toward a superman complex. Maybe your unconscious mind leads you in that direction. Maybe you can blame it on your upbringing. I think I was blessed with all three, if blessed is the right word.

But I didn't try to act like superman, day after day, year

after year, no matter what the result, no matter how it made me feel, simply because of my predispositions or my upbringing. My superman complex led me to form a set of habits—and cling to them, almost desperately. I'm talking about *bad* habits here, habits that ran my life—and the lives of a lot of people around me for that matter. These habits focused my energies, but they also limited my world, because I let them become so deeply ingrained.

For many years, I didn't see these behavior patterns as habits. I thought they *were* me, if I thought about it at all. This was who I was, or so I thought. I was a hard-driving guy. It didn't occur to me that I was really a guy who had a habit of being hard-driving. And a habit of believing I could do anything. And a habit of demanding superhuman effort from my employees and my family.

Then I changed. I started dropping habits that were doing me more harm than good and substituting habits that made my life more fulfilling, more interesting, and a lot more fun. I didn't change my inner nature. But I did change my superman-complex behavior, and that helped me change my attitude. And if I did it, you can too.

As you might guess from the detailed description of the superman complex in chapter 4, these are some of the worst habits of people with superman complexes (and remember, few people have them all):

- **Telling yourself you can do everything**
- **Placing blame**
- **Insisting "It's my way or the highway"**
- **Indulging in contempt for "lesser beings"**
- **Engaging in "coulda, woulda, shoulda" thinking**
- **Maintaining your dignity at all costs**
- **Wallowing in impatience**
- **Interrupting**
- **Being a perfectionist**

- **Asking others to be perfectionists**
- **Intimidating subordinates, friends, or family members**
- **Trying to control everyone and everything**

If you truly want to break the grip of your superman complex, you've got some work to do, some bad habits to break. But I'm not going to saddle you with totally negative tasks. I figure that if you clean out some bad habits, you have room to take up some good ones. . . .

> *The secret of the truly successful, I believe, is that they learned very early in life how not to be busy. They saw through that adage, repeated to me so often in childhood, that anything worth doing is worth doing well. The truth is, many things are worth doing only in the most slovenly, halfhearted fashion possible, and many other things are not worth doing at all.*
>
> —Barbara Ehrenreich

Habits to make

Many of the habits I made as my superman complex grew made my life worse—my workaholism, for example, and my perfectionism. But some habits have made my life better. For instance, my habit of analyzing any problem I confronted, and working up a logical plan to solve it. Eventually, I realized this habit phenomenon was not just a problem, it was an opportunity. Yes, I could work on breaking the negative habits that made up my superman complex. But I could also consciously develop new habits, positive habits that would help me be more of who I really am.

Over the years, I've come up with a number of these: new habits, good habits, that will not only weaken your superman complex, but won't interfere with your normal desire to achieve and succeed. I offer them here because I think they'll help you, and I know, from my own experience, that they'll increase the joy you get from life, and maybe the pleasure you give to others.

- **Take time to chat with people who "don't matter"**

Every day, we come into brief, casual contact with people who "don't matter," whose impact on our lives is brief and impersonal: the cab driver, the FedEx guy, the waitress, the news dealer, the parking lot attendant, the supermarket clerk—we all have our own individual circles of folks like these. People with the superman complex usually feel these folks aren't worth more than a passing glance and a utilitarian comment at most. Our minds are occupied with more important matters. We want to do business with these people as quickly and efficiently as possible, then move on to tasks more suited to our talents and ambitions.

I'm suggesting another habit: stopping to chat with one of these folks for at least a minute, no less than twice a day. Focusing on them and not on yourself. Why? Several reasons: it builds breathing time into the day, it forces us to step off our high horses and be human for a moment, it exposes us to ideas and viewpoints we don't usually hear, and it's doing something nice: expressing respect for people who don't usually get much.

Is this going to turn your life around all by itself? No.

But if you genuinely make a habit out of chatting, you'll find yourself more open to people and more comfortable with yourself.

• Tell jokes

I'm not talking about the joke you tell to start off a speech or warm up a meeting. They're more techniques than jokes anyhow. I'm talking about telling a joke one-on-one to a coworker, a subordinate, an employee, your wife, and your kids. (E-mail doesn't count.) My suggestion: do it at least once a week, without warning or ceremony. Let others tell you jokes, too. And let yourself laugh.

"But I'm not comfortable telling jokes," you say. Well, get comfortable. That's the whole point of the exercise. To help you get comfortable doing something easy, informal, and human. To help you—and the people around you—to see yourself not as superman, but as one of the guys. By the way, don't tell your assistant to find jokes for you. Finding the jokes is part of the job.

Do you already tell jokes? Are you willing to waste a few moments producing nothing more than a few smiles? Well, if so, that's a good sign. Now start telling them to people farther down the line, people who don't usually see you relaxed: the guy in the mailroom, the receptionist, the cleaning lady, your daughter's boyfriend.

When you tell someone a joke, you're complimenting them. You're saying you want to take the time to make them smile. You're also saying the two of you have something in common: you have similar senses of humor. Finally, you're saying, "I'm not all business all the time. I can have fun too. I'm a human being."

By the way, to be hired at Southwest Airlines, you have to cite a time in the last two weeks when you used humor on your job. There's a company that understands the value of humor. In human relations, it is the most reliable lubricator of all.

• Shrug at least twice a day

What, precisely, is a shrug? According to my dictionary, to *shrug* means "to raise (the shoulders) especially as a gesture of doubt, disdain, or indifference." It means "So what?"

It's the "indifference" part of the definition that suits me best. When I shrug—and it's a habit I've had to learn—I'm telling myself and anyone who happens to be watching, "That's the way it is, nothing to be done about it." I'm saying it's time to surrender to circumstance, that struggling is not only useless, it's silly.

To my mind, shrugging is one of the best tools we have to defeat the control freak within us. It's a way of acknowledging we simply can't control everything. Better yet, it's graceful submission. It's hard to shrug and still be furious and frustrated. Shrugging, then, is good for the digestive processes—not just yours, but your employees, your family, and your friends.

Worried about overdoing it? Don't. I'm willing to guarantee you that every time you can manage a shrug, the gesture will be completely warranted. Somehow, when you shrug, you feel as though you're tossing the weight of the world off your shoulders. It's surprisingly relaxing.

• Let someone else drive

Here's another way to weaken the control freak within. Let your wife drive, or if you're the wife, let your teenaged son drive. Sit in the back seat. Close your eyes and take a nap. Say, "Let me know when we're there."

Your superman complex habit of being puppet master will not like this. It will be very uncomfortable. Letting someone else take the responsibility when you're quite capable of doing it yourself isn't easy for someone with the superman complex. We're hungry for responsibility, even jealous of others when they have it and we don't.

But if you let someone else drive—not once, mind you, but frequently—you'll soon find that it's relaxing not to have that responsibility. And you'll still get to where you're going, probably just as quickly. Also, letting someone else drive helps you become comfortable with delegating, and it has a positive effect on your appointed driver: he (or she) feels trusted. And people who are trusted tend to live up to expectations. It's an opportunity for them to grow.

• Play golf or tennis without keeping score

Another aspect of the superman complex: competitiveness. Now competitiveness, in and of itself, is not bad. There's nothing wrong with a quart of competitiveness, or even a gallon. It will keep you sharp and help you get ahead. But a thousand fifty-five-gallon drums full may be a little much, no?

What can you do to numb excess competitiveness? Well, what works for me—and I'm as competitive as anyone I've ever met—is playing golf or tennis or going bowling without keeping score. Golf is especially good, because your decision not to count strokes doesn't have to spoil the fun for the others you may be playing with. Let them count if they want.

When you stop keeping score, something very important happens. You concentrate on doing your best on each shot or stroke—and not on beating someone else. A dog doesn't keep score in a game of Frisbee. He simply devotes his entire mind and body to making the catch. He doesn't have a single thought about making more catches than the dog at the other end of the park. He's not even concerned with beating his own percentage-caught record.

I'm not suggesting you limit yourself to playing scoreless golf or tennis. But I am saying that when you do it, you'll find a pleasure in the game you haven't found before. You'll find a freedom and sense of relaxation you've been missing. And you'll be defusing that superman complex.

• Stop trying to do two things at once

How did I know you have a habit of doing several things at once, or trying to? Because it's typical of people like us, people who are driven by a superman complex. It isn't enough to just to eat lunch. We have to multitask, simultaneously checking our stock portfolios, listening to the news, taking a telephone call—and driving to our next appointment.

So what's the problem here? Doing two things at once saves time. It allows us to do even more than usual. It keeps our minds occupied. But it also keeps our blood pressure high, makes it impossible to focus on any single task, dilutes our abilities, and increases the possibility of mistakes (or accidents, if you're acting like a one-man band and driving at the same time).

My suggestion: cut back to one task at a time. Eating lunch? Savor your food. Don't read, don't take telephone calls. Concentrate on the flavor. Driving somewhere? Leave the cell phone home. It's safer and it will give you time to think.

• Read at least one book a month

> *The failure to read good books both enfeebles the vision and strengthens our most fatal tendency—the belief that the here and now is all there is.*
>
> —Allan Bloom

Okay, I can hear you now: "I've got this one knocked—I read business books all the time." Sorry, that won't cut it. When I say books, I'm talking about books that aren't directly related to work. Could be fiction, could be non-fiction. Take a look at the best-seller list and pick out something appealing.

Why am I urging you to get into the book-reading habit? Because I know—all too well—that people like us, who suffer from a superman complex, can focus like a laser beam on the job at hand. Our problem is letting our eyes wander. We're very poor at that. The result is that we tend to be narrow. We rarely see what's outside our immediate field of vision. We don't regularly expose ourselves to a steady stream of new ideas, new values, new questions.

Reading books is the easiest way I know to broaden your vision. But that's not the end of it. Reading is like meditation; it takes your mind away from your ordinary concerns. It offers fresh fodder for your mind. It leads you to think thoughts you haven't thought before. It helps you see yourself more clearly—that's what Wayne Dyer's book did for me. It helps you break old habits. It's also interesting and fun. It gives pleasure. We superman-complex types desperately need all that.

So make it a habit. Stop in at your local bookstore or library and pick up something that has nothing to do with business. Think of book reading as a present you give to yourself.

- **Apologize when you're wrong**

I think Clint Eastwood said it in one of his Dirty Harry pictures: "Don't apologize. It shows weakness." Well, that's a superman-complex remark if ever I've heard one—and Dirty Harry fits the description all right.

Here's what I've discovered in the process of fending off the superman complex: It's the strong man who can apologize. The strong man knows he can easily survive being wrong and admitting it. The strong man knows that he can afford a few flaws, a few chinks in his armor.

True, if you apologize constantly—for interrupting, talking too loud, forgetting how many lumps he or she takes in his sugar—you will look like a wimp. You'll make it seem as though you're apologizing for who you are. But that doesn't hold true if you apologize when you know you're wrong. In that situation, apologies reflect self-confidence, not weakness.

The benefits from apologizing when it's appropriate are many. To begin with, it makes us more human in our eyes and everyone else's as well. Our subordinates appreciate it, too, because it shows them we know no one is perfect, not even the boss. Our apologies give our spouses and children relief and satisfaction as well, because when we apologize—knowing how hard it is for us—they know we're sincerely saying we're sorry. Strangely enough, I find that when I apologize, it doesn't make me feel bad. Just the opposite. I feel as though I've given a gift.

When I don't apologize, by the way, I'm uncomfortable somewhere beneath the surface. It's a feeling I have to swallow—sometimes more than once—until it goes away.

Finally, nothing neutralizes anger or resentment better than a heartfelt apology. How does someone respond to an apology? He forgives. That's good, because even superman-complex types like us need to be forgiven from time to time.

- **Speak quietly, say little, laugh more**

> *I have often repented of speaking, but never of holding my tongue.*
> —Xenocrates

Most people with the superman complex—and I include myself—speak loudly and say plenty, usually more than anyone else. Some of us—in this case, I don't fit the description—don't laugh enough. They take themselves too seriously.

I say stop that. Let's make it a habit to do just the opposite.

Let's not talk so much. Let's listen more. I find that when I don't interrupt people, they often have a lot more to say than I thought. And it's not just gum-flapping—it's often interesting and useful, and I wouldn't have heard it if I'd jumped in as usual and taken over the conversation.

Let's not talk so loudly. That's another way of drowning

out other people. It's also a way of saying I think I'm more important than you are. If that's true, they already know it, believe me.

Let's laugh more, including at ourselves. It's healthy, it's appealing, it's relaxing, and it's damned hard to be tense or worried at the same time.

- **Form new friendships with people older and younger than you are**

Whether you're a homemaker/mother or a business executive, whether you're in the military services or in school, chances are almost all of the people you regularly come into contact with are about the same age you are. They look like you, think like you, and act like you.

This is not a good thing—especially for people like us, people who are already wearing self-imposed blinders to help us focus on our chosen tasks. Surrounding ourselves with what might as well be our identical twins could lead to a bad case of tunnel vision.

My remedy for this: making friends with someone twenty-five years younger than I am and also with someone twenty-five years older. I'm talking about the kind of friendship that calls for lunch or dinner every week or so, the kind where you go to ball games, play golf, or go to the movies together, where work talk is missing or minimal.

There's a method to my madness. When people like us befriend people much older and much younger than we are, we open ourselves up to unfamiliar ideas, experiences, and perspectives. We stretch our minds. And we wind up a little less focused on ourselves, which, for people with a superman complex, is very healthy.

But you're surrounded with people more or less your same age. Where do you go to get friends twenty-five years older or younger than you are? Probably the best source: your relatives, or your spouse's relatives.

• Try New Things

> *They love the old who do not know the new.*
> —German Proverb

People who suffer from the superman complex very often impose strict limits on what they'll do, where they'll go, and when. And they seem to have good reasons.

- *"I won't stay at an airport motel. It's too noisy and I need my sleep."*

- *"A fast-food restaurant—the food is awful and the people who eat at those places are worse."*

- *"Bowling just isn't my sport—doesn't draw the right sort of people."*

- *"Go to a supermarket? That's not a man's job."*

- *"I can't stand going to be beach. It bores me to death."*

- *"Hobbies? I'm too busy for hobbies."*

- *"No, I don't do any volunteer work. I'd rather write a check."*

- *"Indian food? That foreign stuff doesn't agree with me."*

When we superman types say things like this, what we're really doing is trying to narrow our choices and maintain our focus. We're trying to avoid distractions, trying to stay within our comfort zones, sticking with the familiar for no other reason than it is familiar.

This sounds fairly harmless, but it's not. It harms us by preventing us from having new experiences, by helping us avoid new ideas, by keeping us in our comfortable ruts. It's like putting a governor on a Porsche—an artificial and, in the end, ineffective way to avoid risk. It perpetuates our belief that we're superior to other people, a belief that puts distance between us and our loved ones.

So, how do you defeat this habit? By substituting another one: trying new things whenever you have the opportunity. Try a new restaurant. Stay someplace different when you're on a business trip. Eat ethnic food you're unfamiliar with. Go on exactly the sort of vacation you'd "never be caught dead" going on. Take a class in something that has no work value. Volunteer at a soup kitchen or a hospital emergency room or a grade school.

In opening ourselves to new experiences, we find that suddenly we're not the top dog anymore and there's no use pretending we are. We're learners. We're at the bottom looking up. What does that do to our superman complex? It totally deflates it. But it does no harm to our drive, our ambition, our desire to do well, and all the other good qualities we have that become pathologically exaggerated when we let the superman complex run our lives.

- **Slow down on purpose**

People with the superman complex live life in the fast lane. And if for some reason they're not in the fast lane, they're usually willing to bump someone out of the way, or even run someone over if that's what it takes. We're in the habit of moving fast and being served first.

Trouble is, the faster we go, the less we see. The faster we go, the harder it is to connect with other people. The faster we go, the more we miss. And there's an unfortunate corollary to the equation: the faster we go, the harder it is to slow down.

How do we stop this thundering freight train? By

putting a new habit in its way. That new habit, in brief: slow down on purpose. All right, you say, but how? Here's how:

• Drive in the slow lane. How much of your precious time will this waste? When you find out how little, you'll be embarrassed. You can use it to observe the idiots in the fast lane.

• Choose the longer of two checkout lines. Yes, it will take a little longer. That's a perfect opportunity to think, do some people watching, remember your favorite football plays, or simply relax.

• Leave your watch at home. Ask someone what time it is, if you must, but get yourself out of the habit of constantly checking your wrist.

• Leave work early at least once a week, and don't take your briefcase home with you.

• Spend fifteen minutes a day doing nothing, at least nothing productive. Slip a good tape into your Walkman and stroll downtown. Go to a museum. Take a car for a test drive. Play a video game.

• Don't worry about being five or ten minutes late occasionally. It's only human to be late once in a while. It will not harm your chances of getting into heaven and the person you're meeting probably won't be there any earlier than you are.

• Never—or hardly ever—be too busy to chat, play, shop, read, or exercise. Whatever you can do to broaden your life should take priority over the familiar grind. At least sometimes.

What does all of this do for people like us? It gets us

out of our ruts. It forces us to relax. It gets us off the fast track, at least for a little while. It gives us a chance to take stock, to be a little less super and a little more human. It makes life more satisfying.

• Let others decide

> *I've learned one thing in politics. You don't make a decision until you have to.*
> —Margaret Thatcher

Decisions are the lifeblood of the superman complex. Every time we make one, we reaffirm our superman status. We remind ourselves—and everyone else—of our power. We put ourselves in a different category from other people because we are exercising control over them.

One of the problems with the superman complex is that it seduces us into making every decision we can get our hands on, not just the ones our position requires us to make. We decide what clothing our spouses should wear. We decide who should sit where at the dinner table or the conference table and whether we'll be drinking red wine or white. We decide who's going in what car. We decide which TV newscast our families will watch. We decide what color car the family will have. We make a thousand different decisions we don't need to make, decisions that others could make just as easily.

What's wrong with this? We're good at making decisions, at least in our opinion. Who's better? Well, the problem is that we're making too many decisions for our own good. We're overwhelming ourselves with the responsibility for making decisions. We're also preventing others from making decisions, or learning how to make them.

Here's my suggestion: don't make a decision unless

you have to, unless no one else is qualified to make it, or no one else is around. Give others a chance—secretaries, assistants, spouses, children, friends. Going out to dinner? Let someone else choose the restaurant. Your unique decision-making skills are not needed here. Going to the movies? Let someone else make the choice. Driving from one place to another? Let someone else choose the route. Let someone else choose the car color.

The same holds true for business situations. Whenever a decision appears on the horizon, let someone else make it unless you are the only person qualified to do so. If you're company president, you may have to choose which senior manager is elevated to vice president. But you can let your vice presidents choose who's elevated to manager.

Dump all the nonessential decisions in other people's laps. They'll appreciate your trust and you'll feel relieved of the burden. Make it a habit. I have, in my business, and as a result my employees see me as the CEO, not the president. That feels pretty good.

One last thought here: When someone else makes the decision, don't question it, don't criticize it, be satisfied with it. Otherwise, you're still making the decision, you're just doing it in slow motion, and you're kicking someone else in the process.

• Change your patterns

Patterns. We all have 'em. We eat Raisin Bran and drink orange juice for breakfast. We drive past five exits on the interstate, take two lefts and three rights and end up in our company parking lots. We watch Brokaw and Letterman. We never wear brown socks with a gray suit. We have dinner every night precisely at 7:00 P.M. We ski at Vail, never Aspen.

Habits, that's what these are. The advantage of these habits is that they're comfortable. They're reliable—they never deliver less (or more) than we expect. The disadvantage is that they put us on automatic pilot, performing our daily routines on about 1 percent of our brain power, letting us dig ruts in our mental landscape and forget we can make a new path whenever we wish.

I recommend a new habit: change. Take a new route to work every day, even if you have to go slightly out of your way. Eat dinner at 8:30 and see how it feels. Leave your tie at home. Or change your lipstick color. Frequently. Learn how to snowboard. Read the *Wall Street Journal* after lunch instead of the instant you can get your hands on it. Skip the news now and then. Instead of running every night, go to the Y and sign up for volleyball.

- **Be generous**

I'm not talking about giving money here. Donating money is effortless and practically painless. I'm talking about giving time and energy to others—listening, offering help that actually requires you to do something: sending someone a book, getting someone together with an expert, figuring out a solution to a knotty problem, providing transportation to someone who needs it, teaching someone something, sharing your experience—all without hidden motives.

A friend of mine walked into his dry cleaner's place one day and found the owner, a small, Korean woman, looking shaken and depressed.

"What's wrong?" he asked—the first part of his gift, showing concern and interest in someone other than himself.

"Neighborhood kids have been coming in here, calling me names, and stealing from me. I'm very scared."

"Hmm," said my friend, putting his problem-solving skills to work—gift number two—"I think I may have a solution to the problem."

He remembered that a navy recruiting station was located next door to the dry cleaner. He talked with the recruiter and asked if he'd be willing to help. "Of course," the navy man said.

Then my friend went to Radio Shack and picked up a remote device and an alarm. He gave the remote control to the dry cleaning lady and put the alarm in the navy recruiting station.

"When there's trouble, hit the button," he told the dry cleaning lady.

"When you hear the signal," he told the navy men, "the lady is in trouble."

The total cost to my friend: about thirty dollars and an hour of his time. The payback: a permanent smile on the face of the dry cleaning lady and priceless satisfaction for the man who helped her.

What about the effect on my friend's superman complex? Well, his act helped break his focus on himself and his achievements. It forced him to empathize with another human being and brought out a warm and caring side of him that another promotion, another bonus, another sale, another honor would not have evoked. It also left the world a little better.

• Open yourself up to others

People who have superman complexes, and of course I include myself, often travel through life with the windows up and the doors shut. We don't let people in. We don't let them know what we're really thinking and feeling, probably because we think we'd look less super if we did.

Of course, I'm not talking here about positive thoughts and feelings. None of us is all that reluctant to let people know when we feel proud, triumphant, happy, thrilled, or just pleased with ourselves and our accomplishments. But we'd rather take our chances with a firing squad than tell anyone, even the people closest to us, when we feel doubt, fear, shame, guilt, or regret. Obviously, we don't want people to see our weaknesses, or what we consider our weaknesses. We want—even if it prevents us from being intimate with the people who care about us most—to look like the superman we're pretending to be, even to ourselves.

But I can tell you from personal experience that even this is just a habit, a bad habit, and it can be snuffed out by developing another habit: openness, also known as sharing—letting those close to you know how you feel, even when you're not so happy. Especially when you're not feeling happy.

I'm not suggesting that we blab about our worries to every passing stranger. In fact, I think we should be careful who we trust and confide in. But we should be able to trust and confide all of our thoughts and feelings, positive and negatives, to at least a few people: our spouses, our best friends, our parents and children if that's appropriate, our closest coworker, our priest, or minister.

One reason to be open, and it's a good one, is that no one will see you as fully human, as someone they can love and identify with, if you show only one side of yourself: the perfect side. People will see you as a statue, worth admiring perhaps, but not inspiring a hug. The second reason to be open is that you can't expect help or comfort if you never show people you need it. And help and comfort is one of the greatest gifts people can give or receive.

> *There is a certain relief in change, even though it be from bad to worse; as I have found in travelling in a stage-coach, that it is often a comfort to shift one's position and be bruised in a new place.*
>
> —Washington Irving

Chapter Thirteen:
A Final Word

I grew up as Billy Carey, an energetic, wide-eyed, optimistic little superkid. In high school it became Bill Carey, and as I headed to Columbia it was Bill Carey who joined all the other Bills and Williams, of which there were and always are plenty. I like the name—it has an Irish background to it. But it isn't exactly memorable.

In my sophomore year at Columbia, however, I found myself with another name, one better suited to another side of me: the aggressive, feisty, 165-pound, five-foot-eight running back I've told you about.

The new name came as a total surprise to me. One morning, I opened the newspaper to the sports pages and there it was, in a headline: "Max Carey is back." I had no idea what that meant. I later learned that Max Carey—actually Maximillian Carnarius—was the "iron man of baseball," a small but ferocious guy who still holds the record for highest percentage of successful base-stealing attempts in the major leagues.

Evidently the New York sportswriters, looking for a hero, decided to cast me in his image and call me by his name, since I was a Carey. Within the week, everyone was calling me Max—teammates, coaches, friends, even eventually my family.

Bill Carey hadn't quite been a grown-up. Emotionally,

he was a softy. Max Carey was a different guy. He was fearless, a defensive halfback who would just as soon knock you down as look at you. He lifted weights, talked tough, and acted tough. He had one heck of a superman complex.

I became Max Carey, and have spent the rest of my life living up to the name—and trying to reconcile the Max on the outside with the Bill on the inside. In a way, I've changed identities twice in my life—once from Bill to Max, and, later, from a divided Max personality to a whole one.

There's a pretty big lesson here for everyone. You can be whoever you want to be. You move to a new school. They haven't defined you. When you go off to college, no matter what you were in high school, you can be who you want to be. When you get a new job, you can be who you want to be. When the sun rises tomorrow morning, you can be who you want to be. If you're willing to do the work.

You can be your own combination of qualities, ones that are part of you, that suit you, and that make you the best you imaginable, the person you were meant to be. I wouldn't be writing this book if I didn't believe that kind of change was possible.

Perfect imperfection

To all of those reading this who have a superman complex: I know I'm asking a lot of you in this book. Or, to put it another way, I'm asking you to ask a lot of yourself. I'm asking you to rise above your superman complex, to toss out a basketful of bad habits and to adopt an entire spectrum of new ones. I'm asking you to do something I did and something I'm still doing every day. I'm even asking you to enjoy it. I'm asking you to believe me when I say the process of getting rid of your superman complex is fun and the result is hugely gratifying, not just to you, but to everyone you're close to, at home and at work.

Now I'm going to ask you to believe one thing more: Even if you do everything, and I do mean *everything* I've suggested, you will not be able to kill your superman complex. Not completely. Every true superman complex has two main components, as I've discussed: nature and nurture (which can in turn be subdivided into genes, personality types, upbringing, societal pressures, and learned behavior, depending on which theories you favor).

Nurture can be defeated. We can overcome our upbringing, we can resist social pressures. We can change the habits these two forces have led us to develop. We can alter our behavior by becoming aware of it and by choosing to act differently, eventually creating new habits.

But we can never completely defeat nature. To the extent that our superman complex behavior is in our genes, it will stay in our genes no matter what we do. If we are addictive personalities, for instance, and we become addicted to achievement, we may be able to break the specific addiction. But we will still be addictive personalities.

You can add saddlebags to a motorcycle, you can change the tires, you can put on a windshield and a CD player and padded arms for the rear seat, but you'll never be able to turn it into a car. You'll never be able to make it into something that *violates* its creator's original intent. Likewise with human beings. Likewise with yourself.

Have I just spent an entire book trying to convince you to do something that's inherently impossible? No. I *know* you can change enough to improve your life dramatically.

Just don't take yourself to task for not being perfect, or not squelching your superman complex completely. It's quite possible, especially for people with the superman complex, to feel that if they haven't entirely eradicated it, they might as well give up the whole thing, like the dieter who breaks his vow by eating a single piece of chocolate and winds up trashing a month-long diet.

My point: when there's a fire, don't be an arsonist. Be

a firefighter. Here's how: Take heart with every victory. Give yourself credit every time you swallow your superman instincts and choose to be a real human being. Take pride in asking for help, or letting someone else make a decision, or quitting at quitting time, or watching someone else lead the meeting.

Fighting relapses

> *To keep a lamp burning we have to keep putting oil in it.*
> —Mother Teresa

While you can't kill your superman complex, you *can* put it to sleep. You can force it into hibernation. You can declaw it. You can weaken it so much it won't be able to make a fist. You can muzzle it, leash it, shove it in a cage and lock the door.

But occasionally, and I speak from personal experience, you will hear scratching, even howling. If you haven't fastened the cage door well enough, your superman complex may slip out and do some damage. And if you ignore it then, it could repossess you, and you might have to start all over again to tame it.

So once you've got your superman complex under control, the first order of business is to be sure it doesn't take over again. That means maintaining the awareness that helped you thwart it in the first place. That means watching yourself and your actions honestly and objectively. That means vigilance.

But let's say you slip. You work too hard. You intimidate family members or coworkers, you manipulate. If you're anything like me, you'll eventually slip in some way. You'll get overconfident and forget about the whole thing.

Then your superman complex will break free and start terrorizing the neighborhood again. What now?

Ever see that arcade game with plastic alligator heads that pop out of caves? You score points—and force them to retreat—when you smack them on the snout with a mallet. Well, it's pretty much the same with the superman complex. When the alligator heads pop out of the caves, bop 'em on the snout with the tools I've been describing here: spotting and acknowledging your bad behavior, building good habits and resisting bad ones, bringing other people into your circle of awareness—family, friends, and other associates—and asking them to help.

Ever see *two* kids going after those alligators at the same time? The big-mouth reptiles don't have a chance. So when your superman complex shows up again, get reinforcements. Herd it back into the cage with the help that's available.

Remission

> *It takes two to speak the truth—one to speak and another to hear.*
>
> —Henry David Thoreau

How can you tell when your superman complex is in remission? Two ways:

1. Ask yourself. I mean *really*. With brutal honesty. Review what you've said and done the last week or so. Think of what you've told your wife. Consider what you've said to your children. Total up how many hours you've spent at leisure. Recall how you've talked to subordinates and what you've asked from them.

Look for evidence—in yourself—of acting according to one or more of the six pillars of the superman complex:

One: The Renaissance man

Have I tried to be all things to all people?

Have I insisted on doing something even in an area of weakness?

Two: The know-it-all

Have I criticized anyone unfairly or harshly?

Have I shown—or even felt—contempt for anyone?

Have I apologized to anyone?

Three: The glutton for punishment

Have I demanded perfection of myself or someone else, when good enough would be good enough?

Have I taxed myself beyond normal human endurance?

Four: The Lone Ranger

Have I refused help when I needed it?

Five: The puppet master

Have I dominated meetings or conversations?

Have I made every decision I could get my hands on?

Have I asked for homage for something I did?

Six: The hall-of-famer

Have I taken credit for something someone else did?

Actually, all of this pretty much boils down to a single question: "Am I acting like a workaholic, know-it-all, perfectionist control freak?" If you're honest with yourself, you'll know whether or not your superman complex is behind bars or out on the prowl.

But just to make absolutely sure, here's the second way to make sure you're still in remission:

2. Ask others. Take aside a member of your family—your oldest child, perhaps. Ask him (or her!) how you've been doing with your superman complex. "Am I backsliding? Am I keeping my promise to you and to myself?" Make absolutely sure he knows you really want the truth, the whole truth, and nothing but the truth and won't get punished for telling it. Then do the same thing with your best friend. And after that, do the same with your closest work colleague.

Much as you ask for the truth, the chances are you'll only get vague reassurances if you don't ask some specific questions, such as these:

- Do I seem more relaxed lately? Do you feel relaxed with me? Do I seem to be enjoying my life more? Do you feel I have time for you?

- Do you think I'm as impatient as ever? Have you noticed me waiting without fidgeting, or driving more reasonably?

- Am I still trying to make your decisions as well as mine? Are you leery about saying something you think will trigger my disagreement? Do you feel more free to run your life or do your job the way you think best?

- Do you feel I'm easier to talk to? Do I really listen to you? Do I respect what you have to say? Or do you feel you have to perform?

- Am I just as stubborn as ever? Have I shown any willingness to compromise or give in? Have I resisted enforcing my will?

- Am I less of a critic than I used to be? Do you feel you can do something without fearing that I'll find

fault with you or embarrass you in front of others?
- How am I treating people these days? Have I been giving others respect? Have I been resisting the urge to intimidate? Have I been friendly, approachable, thoughtful?

Encourage long answers and listen to them. Don't let your family, your friends, your coworkers soft-soap you. You're not looking for kindness here, you're looking for truth—because it's very difficult to deal with reality if you don't know what it is.

OK, so now what? Is it enough to be sure you're making progress, that you're heading in the right direction? Maybe. But if you want to cover all the bases, do that self-inventory in chapter 9 every so often—twice a year perhaps. If you do, my guess is that you'll find your assets are increasing and your liabilities are shrinking.

Payoffs

What do you get if you do all this? What makes the work worthwhile?

If my personal experience—and the experiences of other people I've known who suffer from a superman complex—is a reliable indicator, you'll find your relationships with others improving dramatically. You'll find yourself closer to your family and friends. You and your coworkers will get along better. *Much* better, I expect. You'll feel increased empathy for other people, who, you will discover, are a whole lot more like you than you thought.

You'll find your mental health improving too. Fewer negative emotions, greater satisfaction. Less worry, depression, and anger. An increased ability to savor experiences and people. And a lot more fun.

I believe you'll also feel physical benefits. You'll be less stressed. You'll sleep better. You will probably be less inclined to drink too much and eat too much. You'll feel that you have time to do the things you enjoy.

Your psychic health will also be on the upswing. You'll be increasingly comfortable with the *real* you, instead of an image you're working so hard to project—and believe. You'll find yourself more sensitive to your real feelings and your real needs, and more accepting of your flaws and weaknesses.

Your spiritual health will also improve, because you'll be finding satisfaction and fulfillment in new and more rewarding ways—a little more giving, a little less taking. For me, getting my superman complex under control also has brought me closer to my faith and my God. It's allowed me to ask for help and, I think, to get some.

You'll be a more *productive* person, even when you work less, because you'll play to your strengths and get help where you're weak. You'll find yourself fostering the growth of your subordinates, which will make life easier for you and better for your company. You'll have increased flexibility and resilience to help you deal with what always happens: the unexpected.

Most of all, getting your superman complex under control will give you something people spend their entire lives seeking: a better balance in life, between work and family, between business and pleasure, between internal growth and external achievement.

And that, in turn, will give you increased peace of mind. I know this because that's what's happened to me and to others I know who've conquered their superman complex. If you do what I've suggested in this book, that will happen to you too.

That's my promise to you.

Appendix:

Helping Someone Who Has a Superman Complex

Quiz: Does your husband (or wife) have the superman complex?

1. He or she is the undisputed boss of the entire household. (t) (f)

2. He or she is up to *any* challenge: electrical work, plumbing, carpentry, appliance repair, car repair, wallpapering, painting, gardening. (t) (f)

3. He or she is the expert on *all* family matters: shopping, dating, fashion, finance, vacation planning, illness, schoolwork, job seeking, etc. (t) (f)

4. He or she is a do-it-yourselfer who doesn't want or need help or advice. (t) (f)

5. He or she doesn't make mistakes, but is quick to point out everyone else's. (t) (f)

6. He or she insists on signing off on every family decision, even if it doesn't involve him or her. (t) (f)

7. His or her temper is fearsome. (t) (f)

8. He or she requires that the house always look perfect. (t) (f)

9. He or she demands that the children excel at every activity. (t) (f)

10. He or she disappears into the home office for hours every weekend. (t) (f)

Scoring the quiz: Does your husband (or wife) have the superman complex?

9–10: Someone with a full-blown superman complex lives at your house.

7–8: Most of the six pillars of the complex are in place and at work.

5–6: Your husband (or wife) has several superman-complex traits, but they're likely to be mild.

3–4: Almost everyone acts like they have a superman complex sometimes, and your husband (or wife) is no exception.

0–2: Your spouse is not suffering from the superman complex. Check out other relatives and friends.

Does someone in your life have a superman complex? Your spouse? Your boss? Your best friend? A parent? A coworker? If so, you have my sympathy. It can be hard to live or work with someone who has a superman complex. Sometimes it can be outright impossible. If you live or work with someone who has a superman complex, I don't have to convince you that your life would be better if they got it under control. Their life would be better as well, but you'll probably think of that as a side benefit.

The odds are that you and the superman in your life have clashed many times. You may be fed up with his workaholism, his unavailability, the emotional distance he maintains from you. You may be driven to distraction by his criticism, blaming, and putdowns.

You may be irritated beyond belief with his relentless perfectionism, his inability to be wrong, or to admit it—much less apologize. You may be fed up at being the butt of his anger or his contempt. You may be at your wit's end because of his domineering insistence on taking control of everything, including your life.

You may be disgusted—or worried—by his drinking, his overeating, his inability to relax, his impatience, his inflated self-confidence, his inability to trust, his unwillingness to ask for help, his constant anxiety, and frequent depression.

At any rate, if this has gone on for awhile, you probably feel as though you're beating your head against a stone wall. You tell him, "Don't work so much." You tell him, "Stop shouting." You tell him, "I wish you wouldn't constantly criticize." You tell him, "You have to relax sometime, you know." You tell him, "I can handle that." You tell him, "I wish you wouldn't drink so much." You tell him—well, you know what you tell him, again and again and again, sometimes with brief, modest improvements, usually to no effect whatever, except to make him angry.

So, what can you do that might work?

I have three suggestions, methods that can be used separately or in combination:

1. Tell your story, if you have one

If you have a superman complex—or elements of a superman complex—and you've managed to overcome it using some of the techniques I've described, or methods you've come up with by yourself, tell your story.

I find that when I tell *my* story, when I'm honest and forthright about my struggle against my superman complex and I admit my troubles and fears, the person I'm talking to not only listens with interest, he comes right back at me, either with a story about someone close to him who has the same problem, or with a confession about his own struggles. It's almost as though he (or she) has been waiting for years for the opportunity to talk about it.

What triggers this confession, or this tale of woe? I think it's the fact that I can talk this way about myself, and that I am an obviously successful and happy man. In some odd way, that gives the other person permission to match my confession without feeling belittled in the process.

I speak about the superman complex often, mainly to business audiences, but also to people I met in social situations. And I don't think I've ever discussed the subject without having at least one person come to me afterward to tell me his or her story.

If you have a superman-complex story of your own to tell, tell it to your boss, your in-laws, your coworker, or anyone else who might benefit from it. Don't point out the similarities between your situation and his. Put it all on yourself. Be as honest as you know how. And after awhile, mark my words, he or she will return the favor. Before long, you'll be sharing thoughts about each other's superman complex and how to foil it.

But what do you do if you don't have any superman-complex story of your own to tell? I have an easy answer for you: tell mine. You have my permission. Describe what I discovered about myself, and how, and what I did about it.

Better yet:

2. Give them this book

Giving a copy of *The Superman Complex* to someone who has one isn't as straightforward as it might seem. You don't just hand someone the book and say, "Here, read, change your life." That approach is likely to get instant resistance.

My suggestion: mention a review, cite a recommendation from a friend, then give it to him a day later. Or, if his superman habits are already an issue between you, arrange for him to get the book via a source he won't suspect, or someone who won't raise his hackles. You might even consider it anonymously, via an Internet bookseller.

Secretly pack it in his luggage when he goes on a business trip. Or slip it into his briefcase. This is especially effective when he's taking a long plane trip. Boredom will eventually set in and simple curiosity will assert itself.

Of course, some eggs can't be cracked this way. I know that. Some people are so dominated by their superman complexes—and so much in denial—that even if five different people recommended *The Superman Complex,* they wouldn't be caught dead actually reading it. Even in private.

Very often, these are the people in whom the superman complex is most virulent. These are the people who are making everyone around them miserable, who have become expert at inflating their self-images, and belittling everyone within shouting distance.

Short of assassination—and that may be quite tempting—what can you do to help these people? Fortunately, psychology has developed a technique that those who care can employ to deal with people in denial.

3. Therapy or intervention

I was lucky enough to stumble across a therapist who knew exactly how to help me face my superman complex without scaring me away. He gently led me to see what was really going on in my life. I suspect that many therapists or executive coaches have this skill.

If you feel miserable enough living under the shadow of

the superman complex, it may be possible to convince the superman in your life to get help. For many people with superman complexes, a short term of therapy—a few months—can work wonders. The very nature of the superman complex, however, prevents many of its sufferers from seeking help, even when it's the obvious right step. What can be done to help them? Consider intervention.

You've probably heard about interventions staged to confront family members with addictions—drugs, drinking, even smoking. I believe the same technique could help break the bad habits that come with a superman complex. An intervention is essentially a surprise party minus the birthday. And with a better present.

Step one: Gather as powerful a group of people as you can, drawn from the friends, family, and coworkers of the person with the superman complex. What you're creating here is a conspiracy of sorts. So you want to recruit coconspirators who not only see the situation exactly the way you do, but are willing to stick their necks out a bit to change it.

Among the folks who would make good candidates for the team: long-time friends who are furious or disgusted with the person who has a superman complex, spouses on the verge of giving ultimatums, close work associates ready to throw in the towel, teenage children in rebellion, former teachers or mentors.

How many people do you need? Four or five will do. Six or seven or eight would be better. But boldness is more important than numbers. People who are polite and nice and inoffensive aren't all that useful in an intervention. But people who are willing to speak the bare unadulterated truth, people who are willing to risk the anger of the person with the superman complex, people who can be bold and forthright are invaluable, even essential.

Step two: Once you have your team assembled, consult a professional, someone who has staged interventions before—

a psychologist, a clergyman, even a physician. They'll have some good advice. They might even participate.

Step three: Gather the information. Working as a team, create a thorough and accurate portrait of the person you want to help. Agree on how he or she acts and what effect that has on other people. Create lists of specifics. Build a case that simply cannot be denied.

Step four: Become absolutely clear on how you want the person with a superman complex to change, what habits you need him to abandon, what new behavior you want him to take up. At the same time, become absolutely clear on *why* you want him to change. You probably won't convince him, at least not immediately, but you'll give him food for thought.

Step five: Create an intervention script—and outline of what needs to be said, and in what order. This needn't be long or elaborate. A few handwritten pages will do.

Step six: Assign roles. Each of the people who's going to participate in the intervention should have a specific role, and he or she should speak at a specific time. This is not a formal occasion, but it will help a lot if everyone knows his or her job and has a chance to think about it

Step seven: Practice. Rehearse. Run through it a couple of times. Get comfortable as a group. Help each other.

Step eight: Stage the intervention. It's exactly like a surprise party, except in intent. Pick a likely location and find a way to get the person with the superman complex there at the right time.

An intervention is strong medicine. It can't be done by the faint of heart, but may be the only way to reach people who have nuclear-powered, chromium-plated superman complexes. And in their cases, even a skillful, effective intervention may fail. For some, acting superhuman is a habit they're unwilling or unable to surrender.

For most people with a superman complex, however, an intervention isn't necessary. They have all the tools they need to change within them. All they need is a push at the right moment. Which is exactly why I wrote this book.

Camerado! This is no book; Who touches this touches a man.
—Walt Whitman

Note to readers:
If you found this book valuable, or comforting, or just thought-provoking and would like to get in touch, we would love to hear from you. Write to us and share your superman-complex story. I look forward to personally reading and responding to your letters.

Max Carey
4401 Northside Parkway, Suite 100
Atlanta, GA 30327

or e-mail to
Mcarey@supermancomplex.com